ITALIANS
SWINDLED TO
NEW YORK

False Promises at the Dawn of Immigration

JOE TUCCIARONE AND BEN LARICCIA

THE
History
PRESS

Published by The History Press
Charleston, SC
www.historypress.com

First published 2021

Manufactured in the United States

ISBN 9781467149648

Library of Congress Control Number: 2021938359

Notice: The information in this book is true and complete to the best of our knowledge. It is offered without guarantee on the part of the authors or The History Press. The authors and The History Press disclaim all liability in connection with the use of this book.

ITALIANS SWINDLED TO NEW YORK

Poor things! They entrusted themselves to the authorized emigration agencies, paid the price of the trip to Buenos-Ayres, and they sent them to New York. A "detour" of a few thousand miles: See, this is what it means not to know geography.

—Don Peppino
Fanfulla, *December 25, 1872*

CONTENTS

Contents

PREFACE

There is a maxim in the world of physics known as the "observer effect," which asserts that the study of certain natural phenomena cannot be made without changing them. German physicist Werner Heisenberg used a variation of the hypothesis to explain the uncertainty principle, a component of the quantum mechanics that describes the inner workings of the universe.

We encountered a similar circumstance during the four-year compilation of *Italians Swindled to New York: False Promises at the Dawn of Immigration.* We gathered hundreds of records and carefully assembled them into what seemed to us a coherent, accurate chronicle. Although the overall picture was clear, fragmentary documents and missing information forced us to insert ourselves into the restoration by filling in the gaps as best we could. For example, much of our narrative includes exposing the exploitation of poor Italians at the hands of shipping agents and their co-conspirators. Although these operations spanned several decades, similarities strongly suggest a connection among them. In each case, the perpetrators fraudulently recruited peasants from the rural areas of southern Italy, promising them riches in America. It's logical to assume that, as time progressed, one criminal enterprise was transformed into the next. So, some of the exploitive Italian labor contractors of the 1880s may have begun their careers as swindlers in the Italian countryside during the 1870s. Since the malefactors were operating on the fringes of the law, they left few records and almost no names. Much of the context of that bygone era has long since vanished.

However, affidavits given by swindled immigrants still exist in the historical record. The job of fleshing out the details of what happened and who the responsible parties were required skillful sleuthing on our part. We felt it was important to preserve and present this rich, under-reported history while at the same time avoiding coloring our reconstruction with twenty-first-century points of view.

The groundwork for *Italians Swindled to New York* was begun while we were collecting material for our book *Coal War in the Mahoning Valley: The Origins of Greater Youngstown's Italians.* When we began the research, we looked for things we expected to find. Occasionally, we were successful, but more often than not our searches led to dead ends. After a while, it became apparent that discoveries were often serendipitous, and we realized that we didn't know what we were looking for until we actually found it. Unanticipated results like these were the most rewarding. One unexpected revelation stood out above our other finds, and it became the basis for this volume. We were hit by the enormity of fraud committed against thousands of Italians in the waning months of 1872 and into the following year. We were astounded, really. Singly or in combinations, the fabrications of freelance speculators, ticket brokers and aggressive steamship lines resulted in an unparalleled exodus from Italy to the Americas. Rich archives of contemporary journals, national and international, led us to a remarkable story hiding in plain sight. Time and again we found ample reports pointing to 1872 as the dawn of the mass immigration from Italy.

A record-breaking number of these migrants landed at eastern ports in the United States, most spectacularly in New York, where their visible desperation and large numbers generated a flood of press articles. The further we read about this unprecedented migration, the more we wanted to understand the particulars. What could possibly have driven so many Italians to abandon their native soil? How did widespread, amoral practices throughout the process of immigration begin and continue for so long (years, in fact) and with such vigor, even when confronted by the authorities on two continents? Finally, as Americans of Italian heritage, we can't deny that solidarity with these first arrivals in the United States moved our fingers across the keyboard. We feel privileged, as descendants of Italian forebears, to bring this lost history to light.

ACKNOWLEDGEMENTS

We gratefully acknowledge the advice, assistance and support of the following individuals and institutions: Antonio V. Castiglione, Pamela Dorazio Dean, Tom Dixon, Domenico Di Nucci, Francesco Di Rienzo, Melissa E. Marinaro, Emily Randall, Felice Santilli, Patricia Takacs, Jennifer Tucciarone, Accessible Archives, Archivio della Fondazione Paolo Cresci per la storia dell'emigrazione italiana—Lucca, Biblioteca comunale Sabino Loffredo, Biblioteca Digitale Ligure, Biblioteca Nazionale Centrale di Roma, Biblioteca Panizzi e Decentrate, Biblioteca Pasquale Albino, Florida State University Libraries, *Gazzetta Ufficiale della Repubblica Italiana*, HathiTrust Digital Library, Internet Culturale, the Chesapeake and Ohio Historical Society, Google Books, Google News, the Library of Congress's Chronicling America: Historic American Newspapers and the Statue of Liberty–Ellis Island Foundation Inc.

The authors wish to acknowledge the support of GenealogyBank for the use of its material in our narrative. GenealogyBank.com is a leading online genealogical resource from NewsBank Inc., all rights reserved.

INTRODUCTION

On November 15, 1872, the New York *Evening Post* published a retrospective about former U.S. secretary of state William Henry Seward, who passed away the previous month. The piece was authored by his friend Louis Gaylord Clark, whose reminiscences highlighted his companion's irrepressible nature. Clark recalled an afternoon stroll along Owasco Lake in upstate New York, during which he expressed his fear that the rising tide of immigration posed a threat to American workers: "'Not a bit of it!' exclaimed Mr. Seward, pointing to groups of laborers, with the pickaxes, shovels and spades, at work on the Owasco Canal improvements, 'let them come—the more the better: they dig our canals and build our railroads; and, thank God! there is work enough for all and room enough for all and food enough for all.'"[1]

Seward's exuberance reflected the optimism of the times. America was entering the most prosperous period in its history. The decade of the 1870s ushered in a glittering Gilded Age, where vast fortunes would be made. Among the captains of industry were Andrew Carnegie, Jay Gould and John D. Rockefeller, all of whom amassed great wealth and whose successes created the world's foremost industrial nation. The men who labored for them, an increasing number of whom were immigrants, were the bricks and mortar of their prolific enterprises. But beneath the solid edifices created by the big money of triumphal capitalists, tremors could be felt throughout the foundations. In 1872, trades unionists demanded an eight-hour workday, farmers closed ranks in the face of growing corporate power and the superheated economy began to cool. International banking was teetering toward collapse; within a year, financial empires would totter, gripped by the Panic of 1873.

Amid the splendor and vague hints of coming turmoil, the steamship *Denmark* steered into New York Harbor on November 8, 1872. Aboard were 266 Italians, bereft of money and baggage. During the following eight weeks, almost 3,000 destitute Italians would disembark in the city, all bearing a similar tale of woe. The country watched as the great metropolis scrambled to deal with the deluge of helpless aliens. Remarkably, the migrants weren't random tourists. The mostly male passengers shared the same lot; they were induced to the New World by elaborate artifices of fraud and deception. At the time, no one knew the surge that began in 1872 was the vanguard of a movement that, over the next sixty years, would bring five million Italians to the United States.

William Henry Seward, circa 1860. *Prints & Photographs Division, Library of Congress.*

Despite the reigning view that the great mass immigration of Italians to the United States began in 1880, census records and contemporary journals offer a correction. While the number of Italian arrivals topped ten thousand for the first time that year,[2] the event really began in 1872. Italian immigration during the first half of that year was twice that of the preceding six months. The growth continued through the end of the year and into the next, ending with the Panic of 1873 and the subsequent "Long Depression," which diminished emigration around the world. A six-year decrease during the latter half of the 1870s reflects the prolonged influence of the downturn. The conventional view of Italian immigration, regarding 1880 as the birth of the massive influx, is reasonable if one considers that the rate more than doubled from 1879 to 1880. It is only when we take a broader view, considering the uptick of 1872 and the effects of the depression, that a more accurate and complete picture emerges. It then becomes clear that the sudden jump in immigration for 1880 wasn't the starting point of the phenomenon, but the resumption of an event already in progress. What is more, to ignore the foundational decade of the 1870s is to miss how corrupt practices in Italy and labor exploitation in the United States immediately affected the

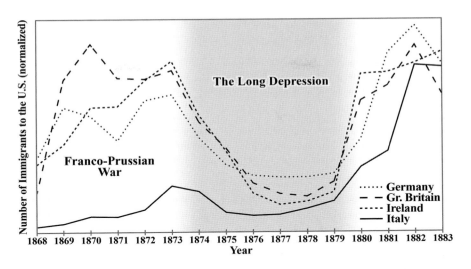

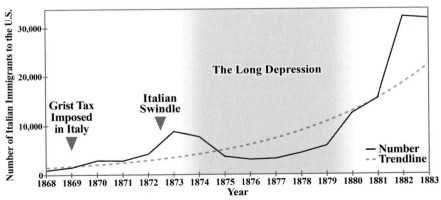

Top: Immigration from four European countries to the United States, 1868–83, showing effects of the depression. *Information from National Archives and Records Administration. Joe Tucciarone.*

Bottom: Italian immigration to the United States, 1868–83, showing the surge of 1872–73. *Information from National Archives and Records Administration. Joe Tucciarone.*

new arrivals and reconfigured the view of Italians as dispossessed victims and dangerously intrusive.

What drove Italians to leave their homes so suddenly and in such great numbers? Beginning in the middle of the nineteenth century, the peninsula witnessed revolutionary changes as political union was forged among previously separate polities. These challenges often defied resolution, especially in the southern area that was once the Kingdom of the Two Sicilies. A decade after Italian unification, crushing taxation and dispossessions left southern Italy in a condition bordering on financial ruin and chaos. In fact, throughout Italy, masses of peasants found themselves in a countryside they hardly recognized anymore. In 1872, the specter of exodus haunted much of the country.

Emigration peddlers appeared in the midst of the upheavals, pitching false and fantastic stories of wealth to be gained in the Americas. Some can only be described as well-dressed and itinerant hucksters who circulated in the hinterlands. Others were ticket hawkers, trusted municipal employees and even men of the cloth. All in all, thousands of desperate farmers and peasants believed the lies and left their families to seek a better life in the New World. Thus, began a diaspora that would persist for decades, eventually growing into one of the greatest population movements in history. The mass immigration of Italians to the United States had begun. Looming large at its origin was the swindle of 1872 and the schemes of unscrupulous shipping agents.

As the United States attempted to assimilate the rush of immigrants, Seward's buoyant proclamation, that the nation had "work enough for all and room enough for all and food enough for all," would be put to the test. Days after the publication of his remark, an array of New York journals—the *Tribune, Sun, New York Herald, Evening Post* and *Commercial*

"Front View of the State Emigrant Refuge and Hospital Institutions, Ward's Island, 1861–1880." *New York Public Library.*

Advertiser—reported the arrival of several hundred Italians aboard the steamship *Holland*. Like their brethren on the *Denmark*, they had no means of support. The authorities sent the impoverished newcomers to the State Emigrant Refuge on Ward's Island, where they were housed at public expense. But American industrialists, hungry for cheap labor, would use the refuge as an arsenal in their struggle with American labor.

The immigrants who had been liabilities were about to become assets. As the economy slid into depression, recruits from Ward's Island were hired to replace intractable native laborers. At first, the entry of Italians into the workforce was met with resentment and violence. Gradually, however, they earned the grudging respect of their American counterparts. Those first Italian immigrants blazed a trail that others soon followed. In the ensuing years, they would dig our canals, build our railroads, pave our roads, mine our coal and forge our iron. They found work enough, room enough and food enough to begin new lives in America.

1.

PRELUDE

An Italian American is any citizen of the United States who is descended from an Italian ancestor. Numbering over 17 million, they comprise the fifth most populous ethnic group in the country. This imposing presence belies the fact that they were not always so numerous in America. Immigration from Italy was virtually nonexistent during the first half of the nineteenth century. For example, between 1820 and 1830, an average of only 44 Italians came to the United States each year.[3] When Giuseppe Garibaldi's army swept through Sicily and the Neapolitan provinces in 1860, a mere 1,019 residents of the peninsula landed here. With the outbreak of the American Civil War, the rate fell sharply and remained below 1,000 per year until 1866.

In 1870, the count rose above 2,000 for the first time and reached 4,190 in 1872. Although it seems impressive, this figure is dwarfed by the totals from other European countries. In that year, for every Italian immigrant to the United States, there were 16 who hailed from Ireland. And Germany, which led all nations, outstripped arrivals from Italy by more than 30 to 1.[4] Still, 1872 marked a watershed in the migration of Italians to America. It was really the beginning of the great wave of Italian immigration that would eventually outpace all other countries.

THE FIRST GENERATION OF ITALIANS IN THE UNITED STATES

The characteristics of the first generation of Italian arrivals contrasted sharply with those of later immigrants, mainly poor farmers, who followed in the mass immigration of the 1870s and beyond. Among these early immigrants, a number of artisans and artistes made their mark. These were stonecutters, painters, musicians and other trained professionals whose skills were in fashion. In addition, they were joined by the occasional émigré who made the United States a temporary or permanent home.

Italian high culture, encompassing the best achievements of European civilization, found a welcome home in the United States, especially among the new republic's elite. Thomas Jefferson employed Italian masons in the construction of Monticello, the word itself from Italian for "a little mountain." Constantino Brumidi's frescoes and paintings, especially those adorning the U.S. Capitol, continue to enthrall. Italians brought to the young, rough-hewn United States the gifts of an educated, cosmopolitan Europe. Moreover, in the works of Rossini and Verdi, Americans found solidarity in the themes of mid-nineteenth-century Italian opera that extolled national independence and triumph over tyranny.

In the field of music, Italian contributions to the young United States were considerable. In September 1805, at the invitation of President Jefferson, fourteen Italian musicians arrived with their wives and children aboard a U.S. Navy ship in Washington, D.C. Among the passengers was Gaetano Carusi, the leader of the group. Since its founding in 1798, the United States Marine Band had specialized in playing fife and drum music for the enjoyment of corps members and the public. With the addition of these and future Italian musicians, a new and more varied repertoire made its appearance. In 1833, Lorenzo da Ponte, an accomplished librettist, founded the first opera house in New York City. These are just a few of the many Italians who contributed to an American audience eager for European music.

The institution of slavery on American soil notwithstanding, European liberals saw the United States as a beacon for Republicanism and a haven for freedom fighters. Several Italians of political note made the United States home, at least temporarily. Among them was Giuseppe Garibaldi, Italy's most celebrated military hero and revolutionary mercenary. During the U.S. Civil War, Italians enrolled in the Confederate army as well as on the Union side. Many in the latter group served as members of the popularly called "Garibaldi Guard," really the Thirty-Ninth New York Volunteer Infantry.

Constantino Brumidi. *Brady-Handy Photograph Collection, Prints & Photographs Division, Library of Congress.*

Apotheosis of Washington, painted by Brumidi on the dome of the U.S. Capitol rotunda.
Library of Congress, Prints & Photographs Division, Detroit Publishing Company Collection.

Another Italian independence hero, Luigi Palma di Cesnola, veteran of Italy's first war of independence, led the Fourth New York Cavalry Regiment in the American conflict.

Early in the war, the North suffered several stinging defeats at the hands of the Rebels. In response to the dire situation, President Lincoln and Secretary of State William Seward made overtures, in the end unsuccessful, to recruit Garibaldi, who expressed a desire to be appointed commander-in-chief of the entire U.S. military. The Italian hero demanded the abolition of slavery as a prerequisite for his service, an objective that was not attained until December 1865.

In the years before 1870, if Americans knew anything about the few Italians in the United States, it would have been most likely in reports about craftsmen, artists or émigrés. In coming years, deteriorating conditions in Italy, aided by technological advances in steamship navigation, would send a stream of unlettered rustics to the Americas.

Giuseppe Garibaldi, 1860. *Photograph by Gustave Le Gray. Courtesy of Getty's Open Content Program.*

POLITICAL CHANGE AND SOCIAL CHAOS

Prior to 1861, the Italian peninsula and Sicily were separate political states. In the early part of the nineteenth century, the idea of Risorgimento, a resurgent, united Italy, gained popularity, especially among the educated and the middle classes. What was to become the modern Kingdom of Italy had its incubation in the Kingdom of Piedmont-Sardinia, governed by monarchs from the House of Savoy. Beginning in 1859, the Piedmontese ruler, Victor Emmanuel II, added Lombardy, Tuscany and the Papal States in the drive to win political unification. In 1860, Giuseppe Garibaldi's culminating military victory over the Bourbon-ruled Kingdom of the Two Sicilies set into motion the annexation of southern Italy to the territory under the command of Piedmont-Sardinia. A handshake (*stretta di mano*) exchanged by Garibaldi and Victor Emmanuel, both mounted on horseback, effected the transfer. With no strings attached, unification forces gained the huge southern territory. A year later, the new Italian nation was born as the Kingdom of Italy, a constitutional monarchy, with Victor Emmanuel II installed as king.

As to the former Bourbon realm, the region continued with the idyllic sobriquet Mezzogiorno, Italian for "midday." But contrary to its poetic designation, conditions were far from perfect, with glaring differences in wealth and resources, some of which continue today. Centuries-old political and geographic divisions combined to make southern Italians economically and culturally distinct from their brethren to the north. These differences would severely challenge attempts to create a united country.

At first, the Kingdom of Italy offered little to soften the blow of political and cultural change hitting the South. As a result, emigration increasingly seemed the only hope of escape. Those attempting to leave were overwhelmingly impoverished men who were illiterate, unfamiliar with English and did not speak standard Italian. This difference in makeup with the previous generation of immigrants affected how Americans would view the growing wave of destitute newcomers appearing in New York and other northeastern ports.

As the political phase of unification drew to a close in 1861, reports of brigandage entered the press coverage of the day. Although the existence of bandits is attested to decades before the unification of Italy, now the ranks of the *briganti* grew as a result of radical changes unleashed by land privatization and new taxes. With the shock of annexation to the Kingdom of Italy, the Mezzogiorno broke out in a series of uncoordinated revolts. From the grist tax—really a hated tax on bread—to the imposition of Piedmontese[5] legal

"Meeting of Garibaldi and Victor Emmanuel at Teano," 1860. *Alamy Stock Photo.*

reforms such as compulsory military service, the countryside was in rebellion. Americans took note and closely followed the events.

In the mountains and forests, former soldiers of the defeated Bourbon army joined numbers of landless farmers—men and women—in attacking the new government and the *galantuomini*, or rising middle class, who were identified with it. Reports of kidnapping and murder generated an avid readership of the U.S. press. The grisly news dispatches continued as Rome responded with an iron hand, while remnants of the old order and the Vatican gave moral support to the brigands.

With the onset of extremely bad economic times, several bandit groups organized to take justice into their own hands, often pillaging and kidnapping along the way. In response, King Victor Emmanuel II sent 100,000 troops to subdue the rebellious territory. His soldiers killed thousands, among them many innocents. In the South, Carmine Crocco, one of the most notorious of the brigands, organized a guerrilla army of 2,000 to attack the newly formed country. Crocco's Army and other highwaymen were a danger to public safety and responsible for committing atrocities. People stayed inside behind barred doors.

"Full-length portrait of a bandit in traditional Ciociaria dress," circa 1875.
Alinari Archives.

The August 1866 issue of *Harper's Magazine* carried a ten-page review of William John Charles Moens's "Three Months with Italian Brigands." The story created a romanticized image of Italian outlaws for the American reading public. It described the capture of British traveler William Moens by captain Gaetano Manzo and his troop of briganti. Manzo was cast as a gentlemanly rogue who treated his captive with civility. When Moens's ransom had been secured, Manzo collected a few coins from his comrades so that when he was freed, Moens could "go to Naples like a gentleman."[6] As Moens was released, Manzo extended his hand in friendship. Other, less favorable accounts of brigandage reached readers, painting the ruffians with brutish strokes:

> *The real brigand is a brutal, ignorant, stolid murderer—eating coarse food, sleeping on the ground in all weathers, chased from place to place, with no rest, wretched, ragged, and probably rheumatic. He certainly can lay no claim to be a hero. Generally he is content with sharing the frugal meal of some frightened peasant, and stealing small sums from native travelers. Occasionally, however, larger prey is captured. The brigand Manzi, of the province of Salerno, has just seized a Signor Marcusi, and refuses 100,000 francs ransom for him....It appears strange that such a state of affairs should continue to exist in the midst of civilized Europe.*[7]

As immigration from Italy increased in the early 1870s, the American reading public followed these accounts of widespread disorder taking place in the former Bourbon kingdom. Increasingly, Americans wondered how the United States would assimilate the oddly foreign Italians, economic refugees now spilling into the Port of New York.

THE DRIVERS OF MASS ITALIAN EMIGRATION

In pre-unitary Italy, especially in the old southern kingdom, schooling for peasants and agricultural laborers was rare. Under the educational program of the new regime, Parliament provided that schools be constructed throughout the Kingdom of Italy. But for many decades, *analfabetismo*, or illiteracy, reigned in the adult population. So, how to think of the Italians who boarded ships bound for the Americas in the last months of 1872? Were these ships of fools and gullible dullards? Or did the passengers have cause to abandon their country, only to unwittingly put their fates in the hands of land grifters, profiteers and risky sea vessels? What was happening in newly united Italy that motivated Italians to depart for northern Europe and the Americas? The following is a summary of major factors driving emigration in the 1870s. Notably, the provinces of the vanquished Bourbon regime were the regions that fed Italian emigration to the United States.

A Rising Social Class and Radical Changes in Land Ownership

The newly established and heavily indebted Kingdom of Italy saw opportunity to extract value from previously unalienable land to create a modern state. These were fields, pastures and woodlands whose titles were held by feudal barons and other aristocrats, churches and religious houses and villages. For centuries, farmers and other tenants had possessed the right of usage, in some cases by *usu fructu*, or free right, in others by paying a tax or rent. These properties were not on the real estate market. In 1863, the Italian government passed legislation to convert church-owned lands to securities for public sale. It was one of several reforms designed to integrate the southern provinces into the newly unified nation, pay off government debt and open a land market to small farmers. Under French rule, former city states in central and northern Italy had already begun the process of transforming land into a commodity. By the next decade, the program begun in 1863 was generally failing in the South as a broad land reform measure and would continue doing so in the following decades. But the process did favor the new middle class, which gained wealth and land titles from the changed social relations built on the demise of the old feudal system.

This new group rose through the Risorgimento, Italian for "rising again." This symbolic ideal embodied the desire for national unity in an Italy historically governed by a patchwork of states, domestic and foreign. In many areas, the *galantuomini* bested the traditional elites, the nobles and barons, who by title had previously controlled land and the centers of power. The new social class on the scene was enterprising, innovative and sought to organize the economy to its needs. Inheritance law, standardization of weights and measures, scientific methods of agriculture and a parliamentary form of government—all fruits of French influence—added to their ascendancy. The new players' impact in the countryside amounted to a radical change in land ownership. In fact, an examination of their role is key to understanding the era.

For herdsmen, feudal ordinances granted them use of pastures and free passage for their flocks on public thoroughfares throughout southern Italy. The innovations creating a market economy put this rural labor force in dire straits. Rial points out, "For the peasantry the loss of customary rights and the enclosure of common land was a devastating blow which left them without resource to a water supply, grazing for their animals, or wood for fuel."[8] According to Robert F. Foerster, when asked why they emigrated from Italy, some peasants were said to have replied, "We should have eaten each other had we stayed."[9]

The goal of expropriating ecclesiastical properties and baronial estates for the purpose of putting them up for sale created a real estate market that only the richest peasants could take advantage of. Land now became a commodity that responded to cash, not tradition, and those buying it achieved rising status in the new economy. Because access to tillable soil was basic to survival, the move from feudalism to market-oriented economies of scale opened opportunities for some but put others at grave risk of losing their livelihood. Thus, the break with centuries-old farming and livestock relationships marks a significant driver of emigration, especially from provinces that were once part of the Kingdom of the Two Sicilies.

Denis Mack Smith, a leading scholar of Italian history, describes the new situation. "The landowners no longer had a paternalistic government to keep them in check. One result of the Risorgimento was that the landholding classes became more powerful than ever: they were the electors; they controlled local government; their wishes decided the appointment to jobs, the apportionment of local taxes and public works and public works contracts."[10]

STARTING AT DIFFERENT TIMES and under local conditions, privatization of commons and other feudal properties happened in many parts of Europe, not only in Italy. In notable places on the continent, the resulting changes in land tenure produced a rising middle class. In England, for example, the government of Henry VIII expropriated church lands and handed these over to the barons. Beginning around the start of the 1600s, open fields that had once been village property were fenced in and deeded to individuals.

In France, ecclesiastical lands were auctioned off as part of the revolution. The outcome seems to have enriched the traditional holders of power. "Rather, the redistribution of Church land likely sustained the inequality inherited from the Old Regime which turned out to be conducive to productivity in the agricultural sector in the 19th century when growth was primarily driven by physical capital accumulation."[11]

Importantly, the new conditions in the countryside separated many in the rural landscape psychologically and emotionally from the land. Ellen Rosenman remarks about the effects of enclosure on the British farmer, but it might also have applied to the poor *contadino*, since he and his family were confronted with a very similar loss. "Added to this sense of dislocation was the loss of a specific kind of personhood—or more accurately, manhood—defined by self-reliance, industry, and the ability to support a family. National identity itself was at risk; with the betrayal of a foundational culture, the land itself is dying."[12] Many dependent small farmers faced erasure from the countryside.

The disappearance of these common pastures and fields also hurt the sheepherding trade. For the inhabitants of the southern Apennines, it was the *transumanza*, or seasonal movement to winter grazing lands, that had created a centuries-old economy based on the derivative industries of outfitting, cheese making, provisioning herdsmen and providing lodging. Sheepherding had created the wealth that underpinned that region of the country, not agriculture.

Peasants on a rocky outcrop above Sorrento, circa 1861–80. *Browning Collection, Prints & Photographs Division, Library of Congress.*

In the mid-1800s, the once dominant sheep economy that had nurtured towns along the spine of the Apennines continued to decline. The introduction of agriculture into the rich grazing lands of the Tavoliere delle Puglie, the Plain of Puglia, dealt seasonal sheepherding a serious blow. Plant varieties from the New World, such as corn, and new varieties of legumes introduced a cash crop economy where previously raising and transporting sheep had held sway. The verdant plain became divided into large agricultural estates that no longer welcomed hordes of sheep grazing on their lands, as they had done for seven hundred years.[13] Laws enacted on February 25, 1865, and May 25, 1876, absorbed the royal lands of Tavoliere delle Puglie into the real estate market and abrogated the previous rights of use. Stewart and Mountgarret describe a "terrible misery" that fell on Italy wherever the Kingdom of Italy sold off royal and ecclesiastical lands. According to the authors, the economic program of the newly united Italy was "essentially an asset-stripper."[14]

Left with declining opportunities, former shepherds tried farming near their hometowns. Those living at high elevations in the Southern Apennines found little success. For many towns and villages, the high altitudes did not support traditional Mediterranean crops. Sharecropping and work as a *bracciante*, or hired hand, held little hope where agriculture was so limited. A saying from the town of Capracotta, situated in the High Molise, sums up the stark choices left after the collapse of the transumanza: "One becomes either a brigand or an emigrant."[15]

Taxation

In the first five years of its existence, what would become the Kingdom of Italy waged three wars of independence. As a result of the third such conflict, the Veneto was annexed to the emerging nation state. The government had quadrupled the Italian army to 400,000 soldiers and constructed a first-class naval fleet of ironclad vessels to win the long-sought historical and cultural prize.[16] Not surprisingly, military expenditure added heavily to the national debt of united Italy. Between 1861 and 1864, the deficit stood at almost half of state expenditures, and by 1866, it was over 60 percent.[17] Taxes had to be levied and strategies designed to pay the large debt.

A key feature of post-unification fiscal policy was to tax every region of the country at the same rate, regardless of disparities in wealth. As part of implementing the plan, the royal government imposed a levy on all milled

Anno I.   MARTEDÌ, 25 Giugno 1872.   Num. 2.

IL LADRO

Giornale democratico-sociale.

Tax collectors accosting a peasant. *From the masthead of* Il Ladro, *June 25, 1872. Courtesy of the Library of the Lelio and Lisli Basso Foundation.*

consumables, the *macinato*, or grist tax. The poorer sections of the country fared the worst in what was correctly perceived as an indirect tax on bread. The 1868 tax applied not only to grains such as wheat and barley but also to staples such as peas, beans and other legumes. The measure generated riots as soon as it was imposed.

William A. Douglass, in his classic study of post-unification Agnone, states, "Even more ominous for the lower classes were the successful efforts of the newly propertied, politically powerful galantuomini, to shift the tax burden off the land and onto the consumer." The galantuomini heavily invested in the real estate market.[18] In the south, by 1880, 5 million acres had been sold. Clearly, it was to the advantage of the new elites to avoid taxing the land that formed the basis of their wealth.

In the push to develop the newly founded kingdom, the government promoted various projects, with improvement in literacy and education important targets. Rather than assist poorer regions, such as the Mezzogiorno, in achieving the goal of universal primary education, the law mandated that municipalities of more than four thousand fund instruction from the local treasury.[19] In many impoverished towns, no funds existed to achieve this ambitious goal. It was clear to many that southern Italy, at least with regard to taxation, would not receive assistance from the central government. Among European countries of this era, Italy was the most heavily taxed despite the obvious damage to its economic health.[20]

Adverse Changes in the Landscape

Though less cited by studies of immigration, harmful changes to the environment added to the woes that pushed Italians to the shores of the United States in the early 1870s. Several writers with interest on the subject, such as Denis Mack Smith, Frank M. Snowden and Robert F. Foerster, comment on the destruction of the landscape, especially on the results of deforestation and its causes.

With the mountainous spine of the Apennines extending nearly the entire length of the Italian peninsula, navigable waterways are few, with the Po River one of the exceptions. In the mountains, seasonal torrents create a topography of unstable highlands and hillsides. The violent hydrology of the peninsula has been a perennial problem. Human interventions such as unauthorized construction on weak hills still create risks for woodlands. But the damage to the environment began well before the modern era. For centuries, Italy had experienced deforestation resulting in the deterioration of cropland, pastures and water resources. The Republic of Venice had a constant need for timber to underpin the city and to supply its naval and commercial fleets. Entire forests fell under the Venetian axe and have never reforested. "The Campanille of St. Mark supposedly rests on 100,000 posts, and the Santa Maria della Salute church on more than a million. No one can say exactly how many oak, elm, alder and poplar trees were sunk in the bottom of the lagoon. It must certainly be an unimaginably large number. Not only Venice's Italian hinterland, but also the coasts of Istria and Dalmatia on the opposite side of the Adriatic were almost completely cleared at the behest of Venetian builders. The barren landscapes of the eastern Adriatic coastline still bear witness to this deforestation."[21]

Immediately after unification, there was an alarming desertion from the province of Como in Lombardy. Soil depletion figured as an important factor in the crisis:

> *The causes of this kind of exodus from Lombardy, which recalls very sad times, were frankly revealed by Dr. Ferrario and are all to blame: the innate sterility of that part of the Lombard soil that consumes the vital forces of the farm laborer who works it; the persistent calamity of the dying off* [caused by] *the silkworms; the phomopsis disease that attacks the grape vines; and the diminished local industries that badly manage the competition from outside. All of these contribute to bring the maximum*

Piazza St. Mark, Campanile and St. Mark's Church, in Venice, Italy, 1906. *Prints & Photographs Division, Library of Congress.*

desolation to that densely packed and extremely poor population [in Lombardy] *that has preferred to emigrate, searching for a land more benign and hoping to return with some earnings.*[22]

In his *Conquest of Malaria in Italy: 1900–1962*, Snowden states, "The denuding of the Apennines—a process that stretched over many centuries—reached a crescendo following unification in 1861. Indeed, the years between 1861 and 1900 marked a critical period of widespread and intense destruction."[23] The loss of forest resources, caused in part by an increase in the charcoal trade and the expansion of tillage into what had once been woodlands, seriously depleted the soil. Denis Mack Smith notes that these losses were so great that "a third of the country was to come under one scheme or another of land reclamation."[24]

With the growing exploitation of the soil, incidents of landslides, silted rivers and the spread of malarial waters enter the post-unification historical record. Foerster cites deforestation in this period as a significant factor in the growth of the mosquito-borne disease: "By the increase of the watery area through deforestation in the nineteenth century malaria has been carried into regions hitherto immune, and elsewhere its ravages have intensified. After 1860 it apparently increased in extraordinary fashion."[25]

According to Snowden, "Although the literature on Italian emigration overwhelmingly ignores the role of disease, nineteenth and early twentieth century public health reformers regarded malaria—and the poverty it caused—as one of the major factors that led peasants and farmworkers to leave Italy for the Americas."[26] Malaria also weakened the Italian economy. The disease loomed large in the rice lands of north Italy and the swamps and marshes of the South. Its victims were those who worked in the fields: the *contadini, braccianti* and gleaners, all of whom by occupation labored during the late summer and early fall harvests, the peak of the malaria season. As Italy was a grain producing country, the toll on agricultural production was heavy. In this respect, the disease undermined the ability of the country's cereals to compete on the international market. The accelerated impoverishment of the soil along with the increase in standing water that bred malaria added to the misfortunes of Italians in post-unification Italy. It contributed to the economic backwardness of the country. For many, emigration seemed to be the solution to these two problems.

Underdevelopment

Some have remarked that in the last quarter of the nineteenth century, Italy suffered from a population surplus. Overpopulation existed in the sense that there were too many workers and families to feed and not enough jobs to employ the workforce year-round. This is best seen as a feature of the country's lack of development, a stimulus for emigration. The widespread regions that produced cereals were especially marked by an underemployed seasonal labor force. Once the grain harvest was finished, a task that lasted about a month, little opportunity existed for work elsewhere. In regard to tillers of the soil, evidence indicates that after unification, radical disruption

Italian peasants near Como, circa 1860–1910. *Photograph by Keystone View Company. Prints & Photographs Division, Library of Congress.*

of traditional relationships to the land occurred, especially in the south, where 25 percent of the cultivable area in the Mezzogiorno was privatized.[27] As a consequence, many independent farmers lost access to plots they had always relied on to survive. During the same period, Italy's fertility rate held steady at almost 5 percent each year.[28] As an example of strong demographic growth, in Agnone, in the Molise, population increase hit nearly 80 percent in the period from 1830 to 1871.[29]

Much wealth in the Kingdom of the Two Sicilies had been tied up in land, a strong brake on liquidity, whereas in northern Italy, money flowed more freely and was closer to the older, developed centers of capital and investment that existed beyond the Alps. Clough and Levi cite that Germans and Swiss could be found in northern Italy in the early days of the Kingdom of Italy

"Swiss entrepreneurs were so numerous in Bergamo that they founded a colony"—and that at least one from Germany's Rhineland had located to the Como region.[30] The Frejus Rail Tunnel, opened in 1871, made speedy rail travel possible between Rome and Paris, greatly stimulating commerce between northern and central Italy and France. Stimulated by the increase in northern industry, a self-identified working class began to emerge. Between 1874 and 1876, textile workers in the Piemontese city of Biella struck the area's mills at least eighteen times.[31] This type of united action to defend or even improve one's living standard grew out of conditions shaped by concentrations of industrial production, a landscape not found in many southern provinces.

Naples, as the capital of the Bourbon Kingdom, enjoyed substantial resources and commercial success before unification. The city's gold reserves in 1860 stood at 443 million lire, twice that of the rest of the country.[32] Moreover, the city was a major European center of culture, manufacturing and education, with one of the largest populations on the continent. Despite these important resources, the overall economy of the southern kingdom suffered from underdevelopment. Importantly, it lacked infrastructure. Ironically, 1839 saw the first railway line constructed on the Italian peninsula. It ran between Naples and Portici, a port serving a manufacturing region of iron works and shipbuilding. Yet by 1861, southern rail lines accounted for only 7.2 percent of the country's mileage.[33] When the Parliament of united Italy ended protective tariffs on foreign goods, southern industry fell into decline. Consequently, Naples was hard hit by the loss of its industries. And it lost all of its gold reserves.

What did lack of development look like in the hinterland of the Mezzogiorno? Although the south had several important ports, transportation inland was seriously hampered. The north's Po Valley boasted a year-round navigable river and a system of canals that nurtured economic development and communications. The South, on the other hand, had no comparable network of waterways. Incredibly, even as late as 1890, an estimated 90 percent of southern communities had no connection to roads, having to rely instead on mule and sheep paths. Commerce was stifled without an adequate system of roadways to link markets to suppliers. In contrast with the North, solidarity in the South found expression mainly in identification with the town or city of one's birth and its politics, a phenomenon known as *campanilismo*.

Political and social underdevelopment reigned in the South. Through limitations on suffrage and a lack of instruction in literacy and basic education, the vast majority of the inhabitants of the Mezzogiorno lacked the power to improve the circumstances of their lives. Prior to 1882, only 8 percent of the adult male population of Italy held the franchise, or 2 percent of the population.[34] The peasantry, burdened by dispossession from traditional fields and the imposition of Piedmontese laws, had no voice in government or in civil society to pursue its self-interests. In the South, before the establishment of the unitary Italian state, no system of public schools existed, while the middle and upper classes sent their children to religious schools or hired private tutors for instruction in the home. In the new Italy of the 1860s and 1870s, the peasantry and the working class were far from achieving influence. In the South, even less so.

The lack of unity and representation in parliament stymied necessary reforms, especially when it came to access to farmland. Frozen out of government and muted in society, there was no opportunity for peasants to build coalitions with other poverty-stricken areas to win progress. Consequently, the agricultural labor force of the Mezzogiorno was powerless against ascendant local elites who aligned themselves with the dominant political class in the north. A small farmer didn't seem to have a future, unless precariously as a sharecropper or a menial day laborer. But emigration appeared to offer survival.

National unity came relatively late to Italy. Sharp differences of economic strength and general welfare became evident among the once separate regions, especially between North and South. More than just a collection of disturbing figures and statistics, underdevelopment constrained almost everything. It shortened lives, undermined productivity and worsened deep power differences. One way to measure the phenomenon is to examine how it manifested itself in real numbers. Toniolo employs Morris David Morris's index of the physical quality of life (PQLI), based on literacy, mortality and life expectancy, to reveal these differences. Under this lens, southern Italy and its islands, in 1870, showed an achievement of just 43 percent of the PQLI index of northwest Italy, itself a region behind England and France.[35] At its starkest, underdevelopment can drive an individual from the soil that nurtured generations of ancestors. Warsan Shire's language succinctly frames the dilemma: "You only leave home when home won't let you stay."[36]

The Pull of New York City

Three major Northeast seaports—Boston, Philadelphia and New York—served the United States in the nineteenth century. During colonial times, Boston merchants grew wealthy from the Triangular Trade by which slaves, sugar and rum were shipped around the Atlantic Ocean. An influx from the British Isles and refugees from the potato famine in the late 1840s also contributed to the town's growth. Philadelphia, temporary capital of the United States from 1790 until 1810, was also an important commercial center. But the shallow waters of its harbor and inland location required extra maneuvering from ship captains and some patience on the part of passengers arriving from Europe. The prolonged landfall entailed first sailing south, next rounding Cape May, entering Delaware Bay and then making the final leg of the voyage up the

The *Great Eastern* steamship docked in New York City, circa 1864. *Larry Gottheim Collection, Prints & Photographs Division, Library of Congress.*

Delaware River to the city's docks. In total, it was a circuitous addition of almost ninety miles.

New York, on the other hand, is a deepwater port. After the War of 1812, it steadily gained over other northern ports in commerce and immigration. In 1820, the city's population was twice as great as Philadelphia's. But it was the 1825 opening of the Erie Canal that dealt New York the winning hand. The Great Lakes region and wide expanses of the United States were now within reach of eager settlers and gutsy traders, as the cost of transporting merchandise fell drastically. By 1870, the metropolis counted one million and a half inhabitants. An expanding web of rail lines to the nation's interior would only increase the city's appeal. Its commanding lead among eastern seaports attracted an incoming stream of immigrants. Soon the gentle trickle would crest in an outpouring of unimagined proportions.

EARLY IMMIGRATION TO THE UNITED STATES

Since the birth of the United States, the journey of emigrants to America's shores has been neither safe nor easy. Schemes aimed at defrauding immigrants are nearly as old as the republic itself and as recent as today's headlines. On January 21, 1792, Philadelphia's *Gazette of the United States* revealed a scam targeting residents of the Scottish Highlands: "American Emissaries are said to be traveling the Highlands of Scotland for the purpose of seducing the Inhabitants to emigrate to America…which according to the English paragraphs always terminates in Misery, and ends often in the Slavery of the deluded emigrants!!"[37] Tactics to enable the transportation of impecunious migrants are even older. Just four months after the end of the Revolutionary War, New York's *Independent Gazette* reported the arrival of a group of British servants too poor to pay for their passage to America. The liberty-minded editor proposed freeing them from servitude, suggesting a group of New York citizens should pay the cost of their tickets and be reimbursed via regular deductions from the servants' wages once they found jobs in the New World.[38]

By the early 1800s, immigrants disembarking at the New York docks were commonly fleeced by scammers. Solitary thieves, known as "decoy ducks," frequented the docks and depots of New York, where they accosted unwary travelers. By 1847, the villainy was so widespread that the New York State Legislature passed a bill to protect immigrants. Benevolent associations,

Castle Garden, circa 1865. *Photograph by* George Stacy. *Prints & Photographs Division, Library of Congress.*

such as the British Protective Emigrant Society, were created to safeguard visitors to New York. The lack of a processing center contributed to the risks faced by foreigners; until the middle of the nineteenth century, most immigrants entered the city directly from the docks on the southeast tip of Manhattan Island. A nearby entertainment center known as Castle Garden was converted into the nation's first official immigration depot in 1855. The facility enabled the State of New York to control international traffic, yet criminal activity directed against newcomers persisted. By 1857, as many as three hundred immigrants per month fell victim to swindlers in New York.[39]

THE FIVE POINTS DISTRICT OF NEW YORK

Leaving the dangers of the harbor behind, many wayfarers tramped to the Five Points, a neighborhood inhabited by others of their kind. Situated in Lower Manhattan, the district was named for the five-pointed intersection of Cross (now Mosco), Orange (now Baxter), Little Water (now gone) and Anthony (now Worth) Streets. The community was predominantly Black

"A Tenement House in Mulberry Street." *Illustration by C.A. Vanderhoof. From* Harper's Weekly, *September 13, 1873, University of Michigan Library* and *HathiTrust Digital Library.*

and Irish in the early nineteenth century, but it counted several thousand Italians by the middle of the 1850s. Built on a landfill covering an old pond, shoddy tenements sagged and cracked. Inadequate sanitation and improper drainage contributed to chronic disease and a high infant mortality. The shanties were dark, filthy and infested with vermin. Robbers, prostitutes

"Ragpickers' Court, Mulberry Street." *Illustration by William A. Rogers. From* Harper's Weekly, *April 5, 1879, University of Michigan Library* and *HathiTrust Digital Library.*

and drunks prowled the streets. Denizens of the district conducted dealings under assumed names like "Mary the Washerwoman," "California Butch" and "Roach."[40] Afflicted by overcrowding, unemployment and crime, the Five Points ranked as one of the worst slums in the world.

Or as *Frank Leslie's Illustrated Newspaper* exclaimed, "Five Points! The very letters of the two words, which mean so much, seem, as they are written, to redden with the blood-stains of unavenged crime. There is Murder in every syllable, and Want, Misery and Pestilence take startling form and crowd upon the imagination as the pen traces the words. What a world of wretchedness has been concentrated in this narrow district within a generation!"[41]

In the decade preceding the Civil War, Italians immigrated in growing numbers to the United States. Many of those who entered through the Port of New York settled in the neighborhood around Baxter and Mulberry Streets, just north of the Five Points. The thickly populated area around the "bend" of Mulberry eventually received the nickname "Little Italy." Unfortunately, this colony of Italians would be polluted by the muck and villainy of its southern neighbor. First padrones[42] and later illegal labor contractors would set up shop here. It would become the pulsing heart of Italy in New York and the disturbing nexus of Italian criminality.

An Act to Encourage Immigration

The outbreak of the Civil War profoundly affected the workings of immigration. Thousands of men, on both sides of the Union and the Confederacy, enlisted to join the fight. When farms were left shorthanded and companies found themselves strapped for laborers, the recruitment of overseas hands seemed to be a practical solution to the scarcity of manpower. On June 11, 1863, the American Emigrant Company was incorporated to address the issue. The Connecticut firm was "chartered for the purpose of procuring and assisting emigrants from foreign countries to settle in the United States."[43] To facilitate the immigration of its new hires, the company implemented the idea suggested eighty years earlier by the editor of the *Independent Gazette*. This plan obligated the immigrant to refund travel expenses through a deduction on future earnings. The federal government, acutely aware of the wartime labor shortage, adopted a similar strategy to attract alien workers when it passed

Left: Abraham Lincoln, February 9, 1864. *Prints & Photographs Division, Library of Congress.*

Right: E.B. Washburne, circa 1860–75. *Brady-Handy Photograph Collection, Prints & Photographs Division, Library of Congress.*

An Act to Encourage Immigration in 1864. Elihu Benjamin Washburne, a member of the House of Representatives during the Civil War, stood before his colleagues on April 16 of that year and relayed a message from President Lincoln:

> *I again submit to your consideration the expediency of establishing a system for the encouragement of immigration. Although this source of national wealth and strength is again flowing with greater freedom than for several years before the insurrection occurred, there is still a great deficiency of laborers in every field of industry, especially in agriculture and in our mines, as well of iron and coal as of the precious metals. While the demand for labor is thus increased here, tens of thousands of persons, destitute of remunerative occupation, are thronging our foreign consulates and offering to emigrate to the United States if essential but very cheap assistance can be afforded them. It is easy to see that under the sharp discipline of civil war the nation is beginning a new life. This noble effort demands the aid, and ought to receive the attention and support, of the government.*[44]

Washburne's commentary on Lincoln's address added a sense of urgency to the proposal:

> *The vast number of laboring men, estimated at nearly one million and a quarter, who have left their peaceful pursuits and patriotically gone forth in defence* [sic] *of our government and its institutions, has created a vacuum which is becoming seriously felt in every portion of the country. Never before in our history has there existed so unprecedented a demand for labor as at the present time.*
>
> *In view of the fact that the industrial population of the loyal States has been reduced more than one million of men, who constituted so large a proportion of the able-bodied men of those States between the ages of eighteen and thirty-five, it becomes a matter of the highest importance that their loss should be supplied, and that the labor which they have performed, and which has added so much to the aggregate wealth of the nation, should be replaced. It can only be replaced by the labor of the immigrant who shall come to our shores.*[45]

Responding to the president's recommendation, Congress passed An Act to Encourage Immigration on July 4, 1864. Section 2 of the provision established a system permitting American employers to contract workers abroad, pay their passage to America and deduct the expense from the workers' wages. Such agreements were made valid by the rule, and the nation's courts were empowered to enforce them. The section concluded with the statement that any contract encouraging "slavery or servitude" would not be tolerated.[46] Regardless of this assurance, the U.S. government now sanctioned the contract labor system, a process by which foreigners were bound by what amounted to legalized subjugation.

The flow of immigrants rose significantly during the three years following the passage of the act. At the end of the war, soldiers returned to work and the labor crisis eased, making the statute unnecessary. When it was repealed on March 30, 1868, immigration dropped by 56 percent over the previous year. The act was now dead, but the contract labor system it fostered remained legal for the next seventeen years.

Meanwhile, fraudsters continued to plague naïve immigrants. The outlaws were mainly solitary individuals working independently of each other at the railroad stations and boardinghouses near Castle Garden. But in the postwar years, more devious operatives began functioning on an international level. An instance of this new approach was staged in March

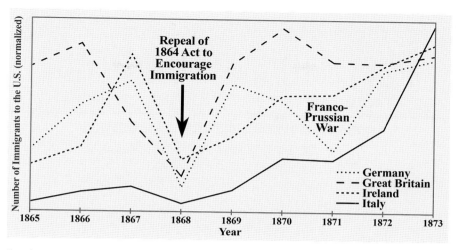

Immigration to the United States dropped sharply following the 1868 repeal of the Act to Encourage Immigration. *Information from National Archives and Records Administration. Joe Tucciarone.*

1870, when nineteen Italian emigrants purchased tickets to San Francisco from a Mr. Bagini, a Genoese shipping agent. He directed the group to Le Havre, a seaport on the northern coast of France, where C. Brown & Company processed them for the transatlantic journey. Upon their arrival in New York, the travelers visited the ticketing office of Boyd and Hincken to confirm the final leg of their trip, a rail excursion to San Francisco. An examination of their vouchers showed they had been overcharged for the transit. Affidavits concerning the affair were presented to the commissioners of emigration, who forwarded the documents to the secretary of state and the Italian consul for further consideration. The firm of Boyd and Hincken had an honorable reputation, and Edward Hincken pronounced C. Brown & Company above suspicion. The blame fell on Bagini in Genoa, who was safely beyond the reach of American authorities. He had successfully carried out an international deception, and though limited in scale, it proved the worth of this nefarious stratagem.

2.

DECEPTION

"A Remarkable Swindle"

On November 18, 1872, the steamship *Holland* entered New York Harbor after a two-week voyage across the Atlantic Ocean. Piloted by Captain John Bragg, the vessel moored at Pier 47, the lower Manhattan dock of the National Line. Of the 789 passengers on the *Holland*, 532 were Italians, most of whom had boarded at Le Havre. As soon as they disembarked, nearly 300 of them converged on the emigration office at Castle Garden. Superintendent Bernard Casserly could see that something was terribly wrong and, with the aid of an interpreter, interviewed some of the newcomers. Certain they were victims of a scam, he persuaded five of them to file an affidavit at the office of the commissioners of emigration.[47] Their statements were taken on November 21, after which notarized copies were dispatched to the Italian and French consuls in New York and the Italian ambassador in Washington. The commissioners also sent a copy to U.S. Secretary of State Hamilton Fish, who included it in a report to the House of Representatives. According to the deponents, passenger agents distributed handbills "in every village and hamlet in Italy" promising that "a great deal of money was to be made in the United States."[48] At Le Havre, travelers bound for Argentina were dismayed when agency employees forced them to board the *Holland*, which was going to New York. Refunds weren't given for the shorter, cheaper trek, and all of the voyagers were stranded at journey's end with no means of support. Had it not been for the promises of abundant wealth made by the traveling salesmen, the Italians would not have come to the United States.

That same day, a telegram was broadcast from New York to editorial offices across the country, relaying the misfortunes of the wretched Italians. Within twenty-four hours, their story was front-page news in the *Cincinnati Gazette*, the *Wilmington Daily Commercial*, the St. Louis *Missouri Democrat*, and the Washington D.C. *Evening Star*. Even far-flung papers like the *Gold Hill Daily News* in Nevada published the tale. But the most detailed account of the tragedy appeared on the front page of the *New York Tribune* in a headline story titled "Emigrants' Wrongs; A Most Heartless Swindle."[49] The paper's coverage of the events was heartrending.

Although three days had passed since their arrival, hundreds of the *Holland*'s Italian passengers still lingered in the main hall at Castle Garden. They huddled miserably around the depot's two large stoves, but the glowing embers failed to brighten their gloomy faces. At the bitter end of an arduous three-week journey, they were penniless and homeless. Worse, they realized the rosy promises that led them to America were nothing but hollow lies.

Weeks earlier, the emigrants had been scraping a bare existence from the countryside when they were approached by shipping dealers roaming among the villages. The peddlers claimed to represent merchants authorized by the Italian government, including Francesco Coppa of Naples and Rochas Padre & Figlio of Turin. The wanderers beguiled their listeners with descriptions of the marvelous opportunities available to settlers in the lands across the seas. Travel arrangements would be handled by the "great Colonization Society" based in Le Havre, whose representatives would greet the pilgrims at every stage of the expedition. Enticed by the seductive presentations, about 280 peasants from Salerno, Benevento, Matera, Capua, Gaeta and Corvo were persuaded to leave for Buenos Aires, where they had been assured gainful employment in a land profuse with riches. For those unable to pay the fare, high-interest loans were offered as collateral for transportation costs. Mortgaging household goods in exchange for tokens, the emigrants departed on the first leg of their journey. Setting out on foot, the hopefuls made their way to Naples, where a ship was chartered to take them to Marseilles. Undeterred by rough weather during the Mediterranean crossing, they arrived at the French seaport on October 31. Many of them had never been so far from home, yet their sojourn had barely begun. Accompanied by proxies of the emigrant society, they now faced a long ride by rail to the northern coast of France.

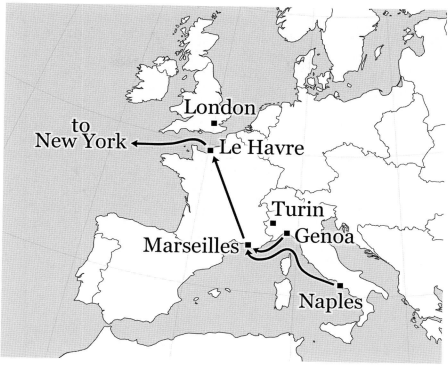

Route of the swindled Italians from November 1872 through January 1873. *Joe Tucciarone.*

On reaching Le Havre, the Italians were informed there would be no ship headed to Buenos Aires for many days. However, it was suggested that the steamship *Holland* could take them to New York, where agency personnel would board them on a southbound steamer at no additional cost. The idea seemed reasonable to the Italians, who were more or less ignorant of Western Hemisphere geography. Besides, with money in short supply, the travelers had little choice but to go along with the new plan. On November 4, they were aboard when the vessel cast off. Two weeks later, the *Holland* reached New York and the immigrants proceeded to the Castle Garden station for processing. Locating the facility's managers, the Italians presented the letters of introduction furnished by the Colonization Society. Expressing steadfast confidence in the organization, the immigrants looked forward to a courteous reception by the society's delegates.

According to the *New York Tribune*, "The assurances of the Commissioners of Emigration that no such society was in existence did not entirely open their eyes. They sat down on the benches in Castle Garden to await the arrival of the agents, who, as they said, were coming to take care of them. They were sure of it 'because they had been told so.' At a late hour last night they were still waiting."[50] As the hours stretched into days, the immigrants gradually accepted the hard truth that they had been cheated. They had been abandoned in a strange land with no contacts and nowhere to go. Adding to the distress, it was soon apparent that the Italians were left with only the clothes they wore, as their baggage was headed to Buenos Aires. Sad faces reflected the utter, overwhelming despair that had replaced the immigrants' hopes and dreams.

One distraught man in particular caught the eye of the *Tribune* correspondent. "Most prominent among the group was an aged father with a large family who clung to him for encouragement, and besought him for some explanation—to tell them why they did not leave such cheerless quarters and seek that beautiful country which they had heard so much about. His agony appeared to be terrible, and he neither shed tears nor offered to his wife or children any words of cheer."[51]

The Commissioners of Emigration were alarmed by the magnitude of the fraud, which was the most serious they had ever encountered. Casserly notified Italy's consul general in New York and the Italian ambassador in Washington, but there was little else he could do to stop the perpetrators. In the meantime, he fed the refugees at the depot and sought temporary employment for the able-bodied among them. He also began making arrangements to send the entire group to Ward's Island, where they would be housed at public expense.

The next day, the *Tribune* continued its chronicle of the *Holland*'s stranded passengers with the front-page story "A Remarkable Swindle; the Bogus El Dorado Scheme." The feature carried a transcription of the affidavit made by the five Italian passengers and included an update on the investigation of the deception. A spokesman for the National Line denied any participation of his company in the scandal and added that their representative in Le Havre was under bond to the French Republic for the gracious treatment of emigrants and the careful handling of their belongings. The duped Italians continued to occupy the main hall at Castle Garden, where they repeatedly begged anyone who approached them for employment. Though sorrowful for the fate of so many unhappy people, the reporter was struck by the stoic appearance of the adults, who were occasionally seen "casting the ends of their huge cloaks over their left shoulders, after the manner of Cassius on the modern stage."[52] The

Steamship *Holland. Various maritime reference sources, Ancestry.*

office of the Italian consulate in New York was jammed by victims of the scam, but the consul himself refused to see them, referring the matter to the commissioners of emigration. For the present, no solutions were offered, no justice was forthcoming and the destitute Italians would be placed in the care of the City of New York. By this time, other New York publications such as the *New York Times, Sun, Evening Post* and *Commercial Advertiser* had joined their voices in the coverage of the episode. But "The Pauper Italians," a November 23 column in the influential *New York Herald*, helped catapult the narrative to national prominence. The epic story of the swindle had become a countrywide sensation and was reprised in dozens of papers from Boston to San Francisco.

Three weeks of relative peace followed the docking of the *Holland.* The respite was shattered on December 9 when the steamship *Italy* discharged over four hundred Italian immigrants into New York. Like their predecessors, the rush of impoverished travelers streamed into Castle Garden. Alarming descriptions of the new arrivals made it into the press. The *New York World* closely followed the growing immigrant wave. One columnist reported that, by day, the immigrants filled the grounds of Castle Garden and, by night, took refuge in the building's rotunda. Furthermore, in their crowded ranks, dangerous criminals took cover. The Neapolitans,

Left: The Honorable Hamilton Fish, circa 1860–75. *Brady-Handy Photograph Collection, Prints & Photographs Division, Library of Congress.*

Right: George Perkins Marsh, circa 1855–65. *Brady-Handy Photograph Collection, Prints & Photographs Division, Library of Congress.*

strangely attired in black cloaks lined in red cloth, appeared to be brigands. The *World* reported:

> *These men, though poorly clad, have the demeanor of a desperado, and strutted back and forwards, at intervals occasionally dropping in a word or two in the low conversation that was going on. They all smoked long pipes and seemed altogether a different class of men from those who sat on the floor. They were altogether differently attired. Some of them wore long stockings of blue or green interspersed with yellow, and pants that came half way to the knee. They seem to be reduced to great poverty, yet show that proud bearing which is supposed to characterize the Neapolitan brigand. Under the cloak each of them carried a dirk.*[53]

Reports of the unforeseen appearance of so many dispossessed Italians were circulating through official channels. Two days after the coming of the *Italy*, the commissioners of emigration sent a report to Secretary of State Hamilton Fish. He promptly cabled George P. Marsh, the U.S. ambassador to Italy, with news of the problem at Castle Garden: "From these papers it appears that a large number of emigrants from Italy have recently been landed there, most of whom were so destitute that they must become a burden to that city. It seems that the persons referred to had been induced to embark for this country by extravagant promises of certain agents in Italy as to the demand for and the wages of labor here."[54] Fish instructed Marsh to publish warnings in Italian newspapers serving the major ports in that country. Marsh did this, and he notified the American consuls at Naples, Palermo and Genoa. He also reported the state of affairs to Emilio Visconti-Venosta, the Italian minister of foreign affairs. Venosta replied with a seemingly contradictory response, promising that his government would do all in its power to stop the deceitful activity while admitting his country's liberal policies forbade its interference in the process of emigration.

Meanwhile, the situation in New York was about to take a turn for the worse. The day after Fish received the commissioners' report, the SS *Queen* steamed into New York Harbor. Like the *Denmark*, *Holland* and *Italy* that preceded it, the steamer was operated by the National Line. Aboard were 437 Italians who, like their countrymen on the other vessels, had been deceived by false advertising at home. But this contingent of newcomers included a new and more disturbing element not present among its predecessors: the *banditti*—Italian outlaws—had come to New York.

"The Most Dreaded Characters"

In the U.S. press of the nineteenth century, the term *banditti* was a common expression for lawbreakers infesting the wilds of Italy, Spain, Mexico and France. Fascinated by exotic lore, Americans adopted the appellation as a popular nickname for larger-than-life villains of faraway lands. When an infamous gang of thieves and murderers terrorized the state of Illinois in the 1830s, it was dubbed the "Banditti of the Prairie." A political cartoon on the cover of the December 7, 1872 *Harper's Weekly* magazine shows how deeply ingrained the concept of the *banditti* had become in the American psyche. President Grant's civil service reform was opposed by Pennsylvania governor John Hartranft and senator Simon Cameron, for which they were portrayed as banditti in this Thomas Nast illustration. The caricature, personifying the desperadoes of legend, was published just five days before the arrival of the *Queen*. When New Yorkers heard that

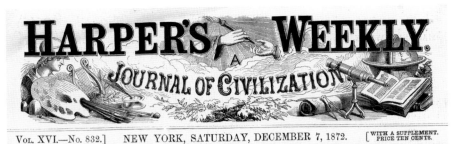

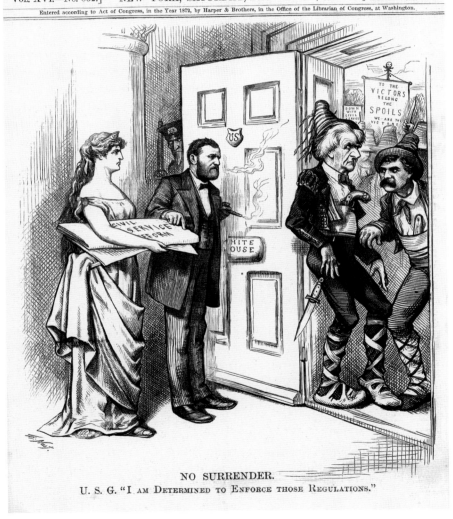

Grant's political opponents depicted as Italian banditti. *Illustration by Thomas Nast. From* Harper's Weekly, *December 7, 1872, University of Michigan Library* and *HathiTrust Digital Library.*

real-life marauders from foreign ports had appeared in their midst, they were both fearful and fascinated.

The interpreter for the commissioners of emigration, wise in the ways of his native land, had his own curious explanation for the advent of this dangerous class on America's shores. Before unification, the Papal government was tolerant of brigands. When the king of Italy came to power, one of his first acts was the abolition of the banditti, so they were hounded across the countryside. Deportation could rid the nation of undesirables, and shipping firms reaped a profit from their passage. Therefore, the new government "opened a path" for the deportation of criminals to America.[55] Upon the arrival of the *Queen*, the interpreter conducted interviews of the incoming foreigners. He stated that many of them were *lazzaroni*, or professional beggars. One of the Italians told him that "he would get his living honestly if he could, but dishonestly if he must."[56]

The voyage of the *Queen* was fraught with trouble. The quarters were meager, and the food was rotten. Passengers were subjected to brutal assaults by the crew. Three people were wounded in as many knife fights, and four others perished, including an Italian who was savagely kicked by a sailor. Another emigrant was left to die, untreated by the ship's doctor. Two more Italian passengers died shortly after their arrival in New York.

Steamship *Queen* of the National Line, circa 1870. *Nineteenth Century American Trade Cards; Boston Public Library.*

Italian brigand, illustration by Grant E. Hamilton. *From Sackett & Wilhelms Litho. Co., April 4, 1891, Prints & Photographs Division, Library of Congress.*

The rumor that the *Queen* conveyed outlaws to America sparked a firestorm in the national press. To the curious onlookers watching them arrive, it seemed as if the characters of legend had stepped from the pages of a book. Peaked hats, knee-length cloaks and striped stockings gave them an outlandish appearance, while the stilettos protruding from their belts were viewed with unease.[57] The sinister demeanor in those dark faces gave no comfort to apprehensive citizens. Information obtained from the inspectors at Castle Garden led a reporter to proclaim, "The Italian emigrants arriving of late, and especially on board the *Queen*, were some of them of the most dreaded characters among the criminal classes of Europe. Mr. Casserly, of the Bureau of Emigration, was fully convinced of the real character of these men before the *Herald* made it public."[58] One commissioner refused to share his findings with the *Herald* for fear it would escalate tensions. But he was too late; the town was already abuzz with speculations.

Prati and De Luca

Despite the sensation surrounding the strangers, New York was already well acquainted with immigrants. At the time of the immigration crisis, Colonel Roberto Prati led the city's small but active Italian community. The one-time Marquis of Rovagnasca, Prati was a lieutenant in the Sardinian *carabinieri* before his exile from Italy. In December 1872, he was elected president of the Italian Republican Association of New York, an organization boasting more than six hundred members. An outspoken advocate of his defrauded countrymen, Prati convinced the membership to open an employment office to benefit the city's jobless Italian immigrants. He also criticized the Italian government for its reluctance to deal with the growing emigration scandal.

On the night of December 15, the association met at the Brooks Assembly Rooms on Broome Street to protest the disgraceful activity. Calling the meeting to order, Prati urged his compatriots to denounce the "horrid traffic in white slaves." Intimately familiar with the political machinery of his homeland, he voiced the prevailing belief that the Italian Consulate in New York was complicit in the sham.

The *New York Herald* reported:

> *There is nothing more humiliating to us than the fact that things look suspicious for our government, and, what is still worse, the conduct of its representative, the Italian Consul in this city, who will give no information regarding the emigrants. They are ignorant peasants from the Southern provinces, misled by deceiving scoundrels, and it is our duty to protect them against the operations of the Colonization Society of which the government of Italy and her representative here are the accomplices. The fact is that the Italian government has for years encouraged and connived at the worst kind of white slave trade in the shipping to New York of thousands of ignorant peasants. And our representative, the Italian Consul, declares that he knows nothing of the matter, and is silent.*[59]

The target of Prati's accusation was Ferdinando De Luca, the Italian consul general in New York during the immigrant crisis. He was caught flat-footed by the unexpected influx of immigrants and the ensuing allegations aimed at his office. He suggested U.S. authorities could stop the flood by speaking directly to the Italian people. "This advice, he says, would be respected;

Above: "New York City—Distributing Food to the Defrauded Italian Immigrants at Castle Garden." *From* Frank Leslie's Illustrated Newspaper, *December 14, 1872, Authors' collection.*

Left: Map of New York City. *From G.W. and C.B. Colton & Co., 1879, Geography and Maps Division, Library of Congress.*

whereas, coming from the Italian Government, it would be suspected."[60] When it was proposed that the Italian government could issue a decree preventing emigration, De Luca responded that such a constraint of liberty was not an option: "'If she did,' said he, 'the press of America would rant about tyrannical despotism, as they have done in the case of Germany and her subjects.'"[61] In spite of De Luca's assurances to the contrary, rumors persisted that the *Queen* had delivered the worst elements of Italian society to the streets of New York. Evidence supporting this point of view surfaced after the foreigners' belongings were searched. "In speaking of the character of the emigrants the reporter stated that Mr. Wells, the Warden of Ward's Island, had taken from the persons of those sent to him a bushel basket full of knives."[62] Regardless of the opinions of his detractors, the consul's straightforward observation on the emigration conundrum bore the ring of truth. "'Allow me to state,' said Mr. De Luca, 'that it would not be necessary for the Colonization Society to send agents among the people of Calabria to induce them to emigrate, for the money that I every week send to the people in that district from relatives of theirs who have emigrated here would be sufficient to induce the exodus you speak of.'"[63]

DECEPTION AND DEATH

For the half-starved residents of the Mezzogiorno, the lure of the con artists was irresistible. As autumn gave way to winter, a growing number of scammed Italian immigrants crowded into Castle Garden. All of them had entrusted their travel arrangements to representatives of crooked shipping agencies, by whom they were betrayed. The most reprehensible grifters were Rochas Padre & Figlio, a Turin-based outfit whose web of deceit stretched across southern Italy. Five hundred forty-nine Italians entered New York aboard the steamship *Erin* on New Year's Day in 1873, all presumed victims of the Rochas syndicate. Among them were Antonio Blois and Giuseppe Roso, who were interviewed by an interpreter for the *New York Herald*. The men described their meeting in Calabria with one of the firm's front men:

> *There was a man came to them, who was also an agent of Rochas, father and son. He had been in America, and wore fine clothes. The people of the district had never seen so grand a personage. He said he was very poor when he left Italy, and all one had to do was to go to America and come back rich.*

He was going to America to get more money, and had only returned to tell all his countrymen that they might secure some of the gold that could be dug out of the ground in that rich land. He got twenty to join him, who sold everything they had in the world to get money to pay their passage. This fine gentleman accompanied them to Turin, where he disappeared.[64]

Michele De Philipo, another passenger of the *Erin*, described how he had been ensnared by Rochas operatives. He was a resident of Calabria, the southernmost region of the Italian peninsula. Like many Calabrians, De Philipo was a poor man who barely managed to provide for his family. Heavy taxes claimed most of the money he earned from the barren, unproductive area. One day, he was approached by dealers from the unscrupulous agency who had already visited several of his neighbors. He said, "They showed us all maps of America and told us all about the country. 'You get rich there very fast,' they said, 'and no one works very hard. You live like a great gentleman (*un nobile*) and work very moderately (*lavoro modarato*). It is a fine country; you should sell everything, even your wife, and go there.'"[65]

At least seventy of the *Erin*'s passengers carried letters of introduction, written in Italy and signed by one Simeone, a bogus shipping agent. The *Herald*'s interpreter translated several of the notes, including one borne by Giuseppe Bardisso, who came from the northern edge of the Piedmont region. Simeone indicated that Bardisso left his family in Italy, and unlike many of his fellow passengers, he intended to come to New York. The letter also suggested the potential for a chain migration that might happen if Bardisso experienced a satisfactory reception. "I warmly recommend him, because he has promised that if he shall be treated accordingly will write to his native village and will induce a number of his companions to come to this country."[66]

In the fall of 1872, an up-and-coming Irish author, Joseph P. McDonnell, decided to immigrate to the United States. At first, he planned to take a ship out of Liverpool but changed his mind when word reached him that steerage passengers from London suffered routine abuse on vessels operated by the National Line. One of these, the SS *Erin*, completed an excursion from London to New York on October 31, 1872. Two days after the ship docked, the *New York Herald* featured an upbeat testimonial of the cruise. Among other commendations, the captain was praised "for the humane treatment exhibited to all on board, from the highest to the lowest."[67] The declaration was signed by nearly all of the *Erin*'s 23 first-class passengers. But a starkly contrasting narrative of the same transit was recounted in the November 4

Steamship *Erin* of the National Line. *National Maritime Museum, Greenwich, London.*

edition of the *Courrier des Etats-Unis,* a French-language journal published in New York City. The *Courrier* reported the abysmal treatment suffered by 114 Alsatian travelers on the steamer. So, on December 5, McDonnell went to London and booked passage on the *Erin.* Departing from London's Victoria Dock and stopping at Le Havre to pick up 750 additional passengers, the ship headed for New York. The eventful crossing would prove a tragic odyssey for the voyagers and a scoop for the aspiring journalist.

From the outset, the journey was plagued with trouble. Hobbled by mechanical problems, the vessel made little headway through the stormy seas. At one point, the rolling waves swept the bulwarks away. The *Erin* was overbooked, and even the steerage compartment had insufficient space for everyone. The crew devised a rough solution by lashing makeshift bunks to the open deck and forcing the Italians into them. For the steerage passengers, the food was often inedible, medical care was practically nonexistent and beatings were a constant threat. Six Italians died during the twenty-eight-day excursion, including an infant born at sea. The tumultuous expedition was briefly covered by dozens of newspapers, but a detailed chronicle by McDonnell revealed every shocking aspect of the crossing.

JOSEPH MCDONNELL, A VOICE OF ALARM

Joseph Patrick McDonnell was born in Dublin, Ireland, on March 27, 1846. As a young man, he joined the Fenians, a revolutionary group dedicated to establishing Ireland as an independent republic. He was arrested and jailed by British authorities for inciting a riot through his writings in the nationalist journal the *United Irishman*. After his release, he moved to London, where he advocated for the release of Irish political prisoners. While in that city, he met Karl Marx, who recommended his membership to the International Workingmen's Association, an organization of communists, socialists and anarchists. During the Franco-Prussian War, he journeyed to France and formed the Irish Brigade, an army unit that defended the French against the invading Germans. Returning to England, he was arrested for violating that country's neutrality law.

Leaving London aboard the steamship *Erin* in December 1872, McDonnell and his wife immigrated to the United States. During the tempestuous voyage, he witnessed the mistreatment of the Italian passengers. Shortly after his arrival in New York City, McDonnell composed an account of the ordeal, "The Ocean Steerage Abuses," which was published in the *New York Herald* on January 27, 1873. The young reporter put the shameful spectacle of immigrant exploitation in front of a national audience. Compelled by a sense of duty toward his voiceless fellow travelers, he courageously publicized the hardships they endured, saying, "Through the columns of the *Herald* I speak to millions. I therefore fear not for the result."[68] McDonnell's exposé drew a calculated response from F.W.J. Hurst, the manager of the National Line. Hurst's blunt denial of wrongdoing sparked a war of words between the two men on the pages of the *Herald*. Other correspondents accused the National Line with complicity in the swindling of Italian immigrants, not only on the *Erin* but also the company's other ships, including the *Denmark*, *Holland*, *Queen* and *Italy*.

Undaunted by Hurst's rebuttal, McDonnell voiced his concerns to the authorities. He sent a message to Richard O'Gorman, chairman of the

NEW YORK HERALD,
MONDAY, JANUARY 27, 1873.

THE OCEAN STEERAGE ABUSES.

Over-Crowding, Bad Food, Ill Treatment and Blackguard Conduct of Sailors.

Men and Women Compelled to Bunk Promiscuously.

A Demand for an Amended Emigration Law.

"The Ocean Steerage Abuses." *From the* New York Herald, *January 27, 1873, Chronicling America, Library of Congress.*

commissioners of emigration at Castle Garden. He also penned a letter to President Grant. Within days, McDonnell received a note from Secretary of State Hamilton Fish, who disclosed the government's investigation of the issue.[69] Encouraged by the secretary's acknowledgement of his efforts, McDonnell continued his inquiries and sent his findings to friends in the British House of Commons. The young journalist had embarked on a lifelong career in which he championed the downtrodden and powerless.

In 1876, he was appointed editor of the nation's first workers' newspaper, the Marxist *New York Labor Standard*. With Samuel Gompers and Peter McGuire, he co-founded the International Labor Union. Relocating to New Jersey, McDonnell helped organize that state's Labor Congress. He also served on New Jersey's State Federation of Labor and headed the State Board of Arbitration. Through his efforts, in 1887, New Jersey became the first state to celebrate Labor Day as a holiday. McDonnell worked tirelessly for workers' rights until his death in 1906. "'Every labor law on the state statute books of New Jersey owes its birth to the fostering care and indefatigable work of McDonnell,' said the *Boston Post* in 1897. 'Not a tithe can be told of all he has done for the betterment of mankind.'"[70]

Italy: Government and Press Reactions to the Swindle

The immigrants' woeful victimization triggered action from the highest levels of the governments of Italy and the United States. Correspondence from Secretary of State Hamilton Fish prompted a response from the Italian parliament. During the legislative meeting of the Chamber of Deputies held on January 20, 1873, Representative Luigi Pissavini proposed that action be taken to prevent "the cruel frauds practiced upon emigrants" like those committed against the recently arrived Italians in the United States.[71] Minister Venosta stated that the government was aware of the tragic situation in New York and was formulating measures to stop the activities of the dishonest organizations.

Alerted by bulletins from the United States, the Italian press broadcast the pitiful state of affairs at the Castle Garden immigration bureau. On December 29, 1872, a correspondent for the Roman newspaper *Fanfulla* authored that paper's lead story, in which he expressed his disgust of the scheming traffickers, calling them *mercanti di carne emigrante*, "merchants of emigrant meat." The *Gazzetta della Provincia di Molise* published two articles about the fraud earlier in the same month. On December 15, it said the director of the Pacific Steam Navigation Company's Liverpool office requested Naples's *Science and Industry* newspaper to publish his protest against a fraudulent handbill signed by one Pietro Baero, a Neapolitan businessman.[72] The bogus circular gave the impression that Baero was a legitimate ticket seller for the company's steamships; however, he was never authorized to represent the shipper. On December 26, the editor of the *Gazzetta* printed a story that had been forwarded by a Naples journal, *La Sentinella*. Intended as a warning to potential emigrants, it mentioned the recent entry in New York of the defrauded Italians.[73]

Italian prime minister Domenico Giovanni Lanza. *From* Il Secolo, *May 11, 1872, Florida State University Libraries.*

The *Sentinella* piece was also published on December 22, 1872, in *Il Circondario di Barletta.* An article about the plight of the Italians appeared on the front page of *Il Circondario* on January 12, 1873. The paper described the bewildered immigrants and the inability of the New York authorities to cope with their needs. According to the account, none of the emigration commissioners could understand the foreigners. "It was therefore necessary to resort to the language of gestures, which, as everyone knows, is used with particular vivacity by the Italians and especially by the inhabitants of the Abruzzi, a region from which most of the new arrivals came."[74]

On January 18, 1873, the Italian government issued an official statement regarding the "reprehensible speculation" driving its citizens to the Americas. Three days later, the proclamation, delivered by Prime Minister Domenico Giovanni Lanza, appeared on the first page of the *Gazzetta Ufficiale del Regno D'Italia*, the Official Journal of the Kingdom of Italy. At the request of Ambassador Marsh, the decree was also reproduced in several other papers, including *Italie*, a French newspaper distributed in Rome. Venosta sent a copy of the French translation to George P. Marsh, who forwarded it to Secretary of State Fish. Brief excerpts from Minister Lanza's lengthy pronouncement indicate the gravity his government assigned to the problem: "A large number of agents travel through those provinces especially where the agricultural population is the poorest and most ignorant, for the purpose of prevailing upon this class to leave their native country, flattering them with the hope of making speedy fortunes in the New World." The prime minister told of peasants selling their belongings to "adroit charlatans" who "pen them up on board of vessels almost like so many cattle," ship them across the Atlantic and abandon them "in abject poverty." He said it was the duty of the government to enforce the law, punish immoral behavior and aid the victims of deceit: "Our consuls have sent accounts to the government of the deplorable situation of thousands of Italians who thus abandon their country, and it is the duty of the government to use all the means in its power to put a stop to this immoral traffic of the agents and to this illegal emigration."[75]

As a result of Lanza's address, the prefect of Turin immediately stopped the emigration of anyone without a written guarantee of employment in the United States. Citizens who had not satisfied their obligatory military service were also forbidden to leave. Under orders from the U.S. secretary of state, Ambassador Marsh advised the consuls at Genoa, Naples and Palermo to alert potential emigrants of the ruse. Milan's *La Perseveranza* and *L'Opinione* in Rome warned their readers about the scam. The report in *L'Opinione* was reprinted in *La Provincia di Pisa*; it began with an utterance of disbelief: "You cannot imagine how many deceptions and how many frauds are committed against the poor emigrants who arrive in New York." The correspondent noted that the victims "place all the blame on the government and wonder how, in a country where a gentleman king rules, such crimes can be committed with impunity. 'There is no justice for the poor;' is the constant conclusion of their grievances."[76]

The *Gazzetta Ufficiale* story was soon a front-page feature of other Italian journals, including *Il Secolo*, *Il Pungolo*, *L'Italia Centrale*, *Fanfulla*, *Corriere dell'Umbria* and *Gazzetta di Venezia*. The January 25 issue of the Roman labor journal *L'Emancipazione* contained a transcription of an article from *La Voce del Popolo*, an Italian-language periodical based in San Francisco. According to the narrative, the Italians who were stranded in New York suffered the bitter cold dressed in rags while piteously crying "hunger, hunger." The author further said, "Anyone who had deliberately studied a means of hurting us as much as possible, who had specifically sought a way of vilifying us before the world, could no more surely have achieved its aim than by sending us these wretches to be maintained by the American municipalities."[77] *La Voce* applauded the efforts of the U.S. secretary of state while simultaneously denouncing the apparent collusion between the Italian government and the duplicitous vendors.

Italian newspapers cover the swindle. *Florida State University Libraries, Biblioteca Universitaria di Pisa, Biblioteca comunale Augusta, Biblioteca della Fondazione Lelio e Lisli Basso, Biblioteca Nazionale Centrale di Roma, Biblioteca comunale Sabino Loffredo, Biblioteca Panizzi e Decentrate.*

The actions of the Italian authorities had an immediate effect on the shipping industry. Advertisements by the French firm Compagnia Francese di Marsiglia appeared frequently in the *Gazzetta della Provincia di Molise* from August 1 through November 24, 1872. Notices for the National Steam Ship Company, represented by the Rochas organization in Turin, also ran in this newspaper on December 1, 5 and 8. But all shipping ads disappeared in the next edition and none was printed again in the *Gazzetta* for nearly five months. The fictitious National Steam Ship Company vanished from the papers, but Compagnia Francese di Marsiglia and the counterfeit Pacific Steam Navigation Company of Naples revived their announcements in *Gazzetta della Provincia di Molise* and *Il Circondario di Barletta* in the autumn of 1873. The following year, Italo-Platense began advertising on the pages of Potenza's *Il Risorgimento Lucano*, hawking its transatlantic passenger service. By the end of 1873, Italian immigration to the United States had exceeded the record number of the previous year.

BRITISH PERSPECTIVES

The British press covered the growing Italian immigration to the Americas with great interest throughout 1872. Stationed in Naples, a correspondent for the *Times* in London provided a series of reports on the development. In April, the journalist noted increasing departures from Genoa and Turin to the Americas, spurred by "exaggerated ideas of many of the emigrants regarding the wealth and necessities of America."[78]

Six months later, the columnist observed increasing emigration through the port of Naples: "I was informed a month since by one who is intimately connected with this movement that 12,000 passports had already been given out to persons intending to leave the country. He had at that time applications from 800 who were coming up from the Provinces bound for other countries." When asked about the causes of the diaspora, an official drearily replied, "Pure misery," adding, "the same causes which send forth the emigrant create the brigand."[79]

In early December, the reporter chronicled a monstrous new deception inflicted on unwary emigrants. Offering tickets to South America, unethical merchants charged clients full price for a transatlantic journey. Unknown to the travelers, the vouchers would only take them as far as Marseilles or Le Havre. The deception was revealed when the captain denied embarkation on his vessel, citing insufficient payment. The stunned victims were left stranded on the docks.[80]

When news of Italians abandoned in New York reached England, periodicals reported the terrible events and reactions of authorities. Several papers commented on the strained relations between Italian and American diplomats resulting from the mess. A rumor arose predicting the imminent recall of Luigi Corti, Italian ambassador to the United States, concerning his supposed conduct during the crisis. According to British newspapers, the hearsay resulted from an unsatisfactory discussion with Secretary of State Hamilton Fish over the scandal. As registered in Edinburgh's *Scotsman*, "This correspondence has ended in a manner offensive to Signor Corti, and he has asked his Government to recall him."[81]

THE ORIGIN OF THE SWINDLE

Records indicate that the practice of defrauding Italian emigrants was already underway at least as far back as 1870. In March of that year, the nineteen

Italians cheated by a Genoese merchant testified that immigrants in some European ports were routinely victimized. Incidents of the kind may have occurred often during the next two years, but if the numbers were small, it could explain why the problem was ignored by the authorities and the press. Not until the end of November 1872, when hundreds of deceived passengers surged into New York, did the situation become noteworthy. While covering that upheaval, a reporter for the *New York Tribune* indicated that the recent incursion was just the largest in a continuing sequence of scams: "Italians frequently arrive here in small numbers, under similar circumstances, it is said; swindlers taking advantage of their ignorance of geography, and persuading them to go to Buenos Ayres by way of New-York, while the passage from Genoa would be a much cheaper and a shorter route."[82]

The naivete of rural peasants coupled with a desire to leave their native soil presented a golden opportunity for grifters, whose deplorable operations began in the opening weeks of 1872. A columnist for the *New York World* noted that from January through November of that year, "a broker at Naples has been doing all in his power to increase the tide of emigration" using "fanciful pictures" depicting the "glorious prospect" of the New World.[83] The unnamed speculator amassed a fortune arranging countless departures. By February, a group of "self-styled benefactors of humanity" located in Paola, Calabria, had organized an elaborate credit scheme for intending emigrants. Groups of ten people signed joint loans that paid for their transatlantic passage. The agreements obligated each cosigner for the entire amount upon the default of the others, and unknown to the subscribers, the ticket price was higher than the going rate.[84] Within weeks, masses of Italians were fleeing dismal economic conditions at home and seeking their fortunes in South America. Many of their comrades were eager to join them, adding to the interest in the growing movement. Unscrupulous agents knew they could purchase steamship tickets to the United States and sell them to inexperienced peasants at double the price, all the while convincing the innocents they were going to South America. Lacking any geographical knowledge of the Atlantic, the hapless dupes were abandoned in New York while the predators profited handsomely by their trickery.

Nearly three thousand defrauded Italians entered New York between November 8, 1872, and January 4, 1873. Those dates mark subsequent arrivals of the *Denmark*, which bore exploited passengers on each occasion. Two dozen of them gave sworn testimonies about their experiences, and since they named their home villages, the geographic area affected by the swindle can be determined. Even this limited sampling of witnesses shows

Locations of fraudulent Italian shipping agents and some of their victims. *Joe Tucciarone.*

that the deception was a wide-ranging affair that penetrated much of the Italian peninsula. The extensive scale of the campaign is demonstrated by the workings of the firm of Rochas Padre & Figlio. Although based in Turin, several Rochas operatives recruited peasants in the province of Calabria, six hundred miles distant.

The February 23, 1873 edition of *La Provincia di Pisa* described the perpetrators of the scam: "Local agents are people of the countryside such as priests, municipal employees and lowly clerks who wouldn't arouse suspicions, because foreigners would easily draw the attention of the authorities and wouldn't be trusted by the peasants."[85] This observation, coupled with the widespread nature of the duplicity, indicates that a structure of fraud was already in place before the *Denmark*, bearing the first-known contingent of deluded immigrants, set sail from London on October 19, 1872.

On November 8, 1872, the *Denmark* slipped quietly into New York Harbor with no fanfare about the circumstances of its occupants. It was only after the landing of the *Holland* ten days later that the press acknowledged the predicament of the *Denmark*'s Italians. In the months preceding the dockings of the *Denmark* and *Holland*, no incidents of abuse against Italian passengers were reported by the newspapers. Yet shipping manifests show that several vessels transported unusually large numbers of them to New York in October 1872. Two of these records document voyages of National Line steamers *Helvetia* and *Erin*; both journeys originated in London, stopped in Le Havre to pick up added travelers and terminated in New York. This was the same route used the following month when National Line ships bore hoodwinked Italians to the United States. On October 17, two hundred Italians disembarked from the *Helvetia* and on October 31, 343 arrived aboard the *Erin*. The *Courrier des Etats-Unis*'s account of the mistreatment of Alsatians on this transit of the *Erin* is reminiscent of the reports of abuse experienced by the Italians on the steamer's next passage. The dailies were silent in the months before the *Tribune* unveiled the deception, yet evidence shows that the cheating of Italian immigrants might already have been an ongoing enterprise.

"THE SLAVES OF THE HARP"

As despicable as it was, the deceit inflicted on the Italian emigrants might have been the offshoot of a far older and more heartbreaking institution: the enslavement of Italian children. The trade dates to ancient times and was so common in sixteenth-century Europe that Spain and England passed laws making criminals of the *comprachicos*, or "child-buyers." In the middle of the nineteenth century, wretched Italian children began appearing on street corners in New York City. Some of them sang, others played the violin or harp and all of them accepted donations from passersby. Every evening, the little ones packed up their instruments and returned to their lodgings, which were usually dirty tenements in the Five Points district. Each waif gave all the day's earnings to the keeper of the household. If the amount was deemed insufficient, the child would be punished. Infractions could include

A free African American and two enslaved Italian children. *Illustration by W.L. Sheppard. From* Harper's Weekly, *December 27, 1873, University of Michigan Library* and *HathiTrust Digital Library.*

denial of supper, beatings or burnings with a hot iron. The cruel keepers of the young performers weren't their parents; they were padrones. Ten weeks before the *Tribune* broke the story of the fraud, the *New York Sun* published a front-page exposé of the young mendicants: "The slave traders are natives of Italy, and generally men who have been to America. The trader travels through the country, stopping at the towns and villages and selecting the

Recruitment of an Italian boy by a padrone. *Illustration by Solomon Eytinge Jr. From* Harper's Weekly, *March 8, 1873, Authors' collection.*

children. France is the distributing point. England and the United States buy the largest number of the children, and it is said that some are shipped to South America. Those intended for the United States are shipped at Havre and landed at Castle Garden in this city."[86]

While New York's first immigrant musicians arrived from the northern regions of Parma and Liguria, from the early 1870s, arrivals from southern Italy, especially from Basilicata, began to take their place. By 1872, the transatlantic peddling of Italian youths was being conducted on a regular basis. The December 17 edition of the *New York Tribune* explained how New York padrones made yearly excursions to villages around Naples, where children were collected. Identifying families with small boys, the recruiter captivated parents with stories of the wonderful prospects awaiting youngsters in the United States: "He approaches the father of the family, and after commenting upon the beauty of his children, tells the infatuated parent that his boys 'should be sent at once to America, where they must in time become rich.'"

Often, the dealer offers to pay the child's passage to America, thus relieving the family of this expense. The parents would receive a contract guaranteeing the safekeeping and eventual return of the youngster, but such agreements were seldom honored. After collecting a number of children, the operator would lead his charges to Genoa and Marseilles, then on to Le Havre or Calais for embarkation to the United States.[87] This was exactly the same route adopted by the swindlers in the fall of 1872. In addition, the agents' mode of rounding up a quota of children from the rural south is eerily similar to the fraudsters' routine of contracting groups of emigrants from the same region. The striking similarities between the method of the slavers and that of the emigrant sharpers demonstrates a possible connection between the two. When the defrauded immigrants first came to New York late in 1872, the system of procuring Italian children, transporting them across the Atlantic and exploiting them on Manhattan street corners was already a well-established practice. By the time Congress deprived the padrones of their immoral livelihood in 1874, the swindling of

Italian boy punished by a padrone. *Illustration by A. Gault. From* Harper's Weekly, *September 13, 1873, Prints & Photographs Division, Library of Congress.*

Italian adults had, in its turn, become a routine undertaking. It's likely that, in the mid-1870s, the American-based *comprachicos* may have transitioned from overseeing indentured children to importing defrauded adults. At least one contemporary source voiced this observation: "Since the exposure that was made of their villainy in importing child labor, they have changed their methods. Where they used to rob, they now swindle."[88]

Consul General and *Capo Padrone*?

Newspaper coverage of the enslaved Italian youths peaked in the summer of 1873, with some newsmen laying blame for the disgraceful practice on Rome's envoy, Ferdinando De Luca. On September 6, the *Boston Pilot* published an exposé disclosing his apparent involvement in the horrific trafficking. In 1864, he was appointed to the consular office in New Orleans. However, the meager salary forced him to borrow money from wealthy Italian residents. According to the *Pilot*, large numbers of Italian street musicians appeared in the United States soon after he was reassigned to New York as Italy's consul general in 1867. At the same time, his finances steadily improved, and he amassed a considerable fortune despite his paltry official income, so much so that he could afford to house his family in a fashionable part of the city. Responding to allegations of wrongdoings, he endorsed an Italian law that would abolish all agreements between parents and padrones. Yet several well-respected Italians claimed to possess contracts for the sale of children that bore De Luca's signature. The consular secretary, Angelo Zilio Grandi, and the office's notary were also implicated in the dealings.

The Rochas Agency and the National Steamship Company

Francis William Jones Hurst was the New York manager of the Liverpool-based National Steamship Company, known in the United States as the National Line. The fraudulent business of Rochas Padre & Figlio of Turin, Italy, advertised and sold overpriced tickets for transatlantic service on vessels managed by Hurst. Although he denied it, evidence seemed to

Caroline and Francis W.J. Hurst. *From* Pinafores to Politics, *1923, National American Woman Suffrage Association Collection (Library of Congress).*

suggest a connection existed between his office and the Rochas operation. In December 1872, the Rochas agency ran simultaneous advertisements in *Gazzetta della Provincia di Molise* and *Il Circondario di Barletta*, newspapers printed in the southern Italian regions of the Molise and Puglia. In the promotions, the Rochas agency assumed a fictitious identity with an English spelling "National Steam Ship Company," a remarkable mimicking of the Liverpool concern's authentic trademark. The ads offered passage from Le Havre to New York and listed the December and January schedules of the *Erin, Denmark, Holland* and *Queen*, all of which Hurst's enterprise managed. In a deliberate attempt to mislead the public, the notices designated the Rochas firm as the "General Agency for Italy." At face value, these commonalities appeared to confirm a supposed collaboration between the National Line and the Rochas bureau. Whether or not a commercial alliance existed between them, Hurst's National Line was heavily invested in the traffic of Italian immigrants to America. More than a dozen companies regularly transported Italians across the Atlantic Ocean in 1872. But the National Line carried more than all the others combined, conveying over 70 percent of all Italian passengers during the year.

From December 1872 through the following month, many among the passengers who voyaged on the *Denmark*, *Holland* and *Erin* purchased their tickets from the Rochas organization. While some of the travelers booked passage to New York, others chose Buenos Aires, a more distant and a correspondingly more expensive outing. A group of emigrants left Italy at the end of October 1872, bound for Le Havre. Before reaching the port, their vouchers were collected by the Rochas hawkers who accompanied them. On arriving at the city, voyagers who paid the fare to Buenos Aires

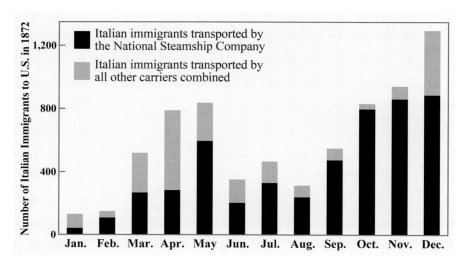

Monthly Italian immigration to the United States in 1872. *Information from National Archives and Records Administration. Joe Tucciarone.*

National steamship advertisement of Rochas, Padre e Figlio. *From* Gazzetta Della Provincia di Molise, *December 8, 1872, Biblioteca Provinciale "P. Albino" Campobasso.*

were coerced by their escorts to go to New York aboard the *Holland*.[89] They were given steamship tickets, and once the vessel was underway, these were taken from them by the captain of the ship.[90] Several weeks later, another party of Italians succumbed to a similar trick. Among them were Giuseppe Budosi, Giovanni Romero and Francesco Negra from the Piedmont region. Persuaded that New York was "a much nicer place" than Buenos Aires, they boarded the *Erin*.[91]

Since their tickets had been honored by pursers on the various vessels, the boarding passes to New York, distributed by the bogus attendants in Le Havre, were legitimate. These would be available from an authorized representative of the National Line in Le Havre. They would have been purchased at the going rate, which was far less than the amount charged by the fraudulent companies for the original, unauthorized tickets supplied in Italy. Part of the excessive cost of that first transaction would have been used to buy the valid tickets; the remainder, the overcharge, would be pocketed by the Rochas proxies. This unethical profit was at the heart of the cruel stratagem.

The Magnitude of the Swindle

Dozens of newspaper articles and eleven ship manifests indicate that 2,908 defrauded Italian immigrants were transported to the United States between November 8, 1872, and January 4, 1873. Although small in comparison with passenger arrivals from the latter decades of the nineteenth century, the historical impact of this event cannot be overstated.

In the last six weeks of 1872, eight vessels carrying 2,057 Italian passengers docked in New York. Four of the ships, the *Denmark*, *Holland*, *Italy* and *Queen*, were operated by the National Line. The other four, the *City of Antwerp*, *City of London*, *City of Montreal* and *City of Washington*, were Inman Line carriers. According to several newspaper articles and one congressional report, most of the Italian passengers on the eight transports were casualties of fraudulent advertising and enlistment drives by shipping agents. American newspapers first sounded the alarm on November 22, yet the influx of Italians began climbing steeply upward almost three months earlier. The pronounced rise was likely the result of illicit recruitments. Many of the newcomers enumerated at that time may have been duped. Manifests at the National Archives show that half of the 7,228[92] Italian immigrants entering the country during calendar year 1872 did so in the last four months of the year. In 1873, the U.S. census tallied 8,757 Italian immigrants.[93] During the first week of the new year, three steamers of the National Line, the *Erin*, *Egypt* and *Denmark*, arrived in New York bearing a total of 851 Italian immigrants. These three voyages conveyed nearly one-tenth of the total number of Italian immigrants for the entire year, and several contemporary journals indicate that many, if not all, were victims of fraud.

The composition of the passengers arriving in New York between November 8, 1872, and January 4, 1873, offers a clue to their intentions. The manifests reveal that 65 percent of the Italians arriving at that time were males over the age of twelve. These men hadn't brought their families on vacation; they were coming to work.

A report compiled by the Italian Ministry of Agriculture, Industry and Commerce suggests that an organized international fraud scheme might have netted Italian emigrants bound to ports outside the United States. *Statistica della emigrazione italiana all'estero*, published in Rome in 1882, listed the number of Italians who went to Le Havre. According to this volume, the figure jumped sevenfold from 1,315 in 1871 to 9,571 in 1872.[94] It will be remembered that several fraudulent shipping operations were based in that

Steamship	Steamship Company	Arrival Date of Ship	Number of Passengers Who Were Italian	Percentage of Italian Passengers Who Were Males Over Age 12
Denmark	National Line	Nov. 8, 1872	266	74.4%
Holland	National Line	Nov. 18, 1872	532	94.9%[1]
City of London	Inman Line	Nov. 19, 1872	62	51.6%
City of Washington	Inman Line	Dec. 5, 1872	129	60.5%
City of Montreal	Inman Line	Dec. 6, 1872	69	78.3%
Italy	National Line	Dec. 9, 1872	444	70.7%
Queen	National Line	Dec. 12, 1872	444	61.8%
City of Antwerp	Inman Line	Dec. 14, 1872	111	64.0%
Erin	National Line	Jan. 1, 1873	549	54.3%
Egypt	National Line	Jan. 2, 1873	113	77.0%
Denmark[2]	National Line	Jan. 4, 1873	189	87.3%

[1]Percentage based on existing thirteen pages of Holland manifest; approx. six pages are missing
[2]The Denmark made two voyages during this period, both times carrying defrauded Italians

Italian immigration to the United States on various steamships from November 8, 1872, to January 4, 1873. *Information from National Archives and Records Administration. Joe Tucciarone.*

port, including the Colonization Society, which was implicated in defrauding Italians headed to America in the fall of 1872. In two other French ports, Marseilles and Bordeaux, officials took note of the heavy expansion in Italian emigration in 1872 and 1873. *Statistica della emigrazione* also recorded the number of Italians who immigrated to Argentina. In 1871, the figure was 8,170, while the number for 1872 was significantly greater at 14,769. An even greater jump to 26,278 occurred in 1873.[95] During those three years, Italians comprised more than a third of all immigrants to Argentina. Between 1871 and 1872, the net growth in the migration of Italians to all other nations grew by 156 percent. These dramatic increases coincided with the advertising campaign initiated by Compagnia Francese di Marsiglia for travel from Naples to Buenos Aires, Rio de Janeiro and Montevideo. These ads targeted southern Italy and appeared in late 1872—twice in August and once in November.[96]

The surge in Italian immigration to Argentina in 1872, coupled with the December 5, 1872 testimony of Abruzzi native Falcone Gregorio, hints at the scope of the duplicity. He was one of the deceived passengers aboard the *City of Washington*, which arrived in New York on December 5. During an investigation by New York's commissioners of emigration, he attested that although 125 Italians left Le Havre on the vessel, they were part of a much larger group of 800 emigrants sent to that port

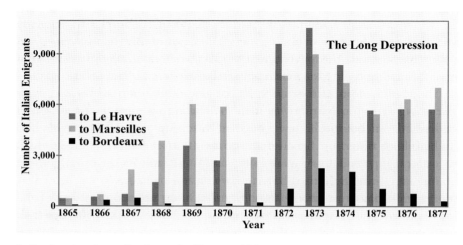

Italian immigration to Bordeaux, Le Havre and Marseilles from 1865 to 1877. *Information from* Statistica della emigrazione italiana all' estero. *Joe Tucciarone.*

by the Emigration Society of Genoa. The entire group was transferred from Naples to Genoa by Francesco Coppa, the Neapolitan businessman accused of swindling the Italians on the *Holland* the previous month. Gregorio indicated that some of the group sailed with him on the *City of Washington*, others boarded a steamer for Buenos Aires "and a few were left destitute in the streets of Havre."[97]

THE ITALIAN EXODUS TO SOUTH AMERICA

Italians watched intently as tens of thousands of their impoverished countrymen deserted the nation in the 1870s. For nearly a year before they overwhelmed the Port of New York in the fall of 1872, Italians were crowding the seaports of South America. Newspaper columnists were among the first to notice the growing movement of immigrants to the republics of the Western Hemisphere. Taking up the cry of his peers, the editor of *La Nuova Basilicata* mourned the dismal economy that was sapping the nation's vitality and driving its citizens to leave: "There is nothing left but to watch the most painful spectacle of the day, the mass emigration to America of peasants, artisans, small businessmen, priests, gentlemen, women, old people, children—in short, every class of people who starve in the land where they were born."[98] According to Rome's *Fanfulla*, 766 Italians departed for the

United States during the first three months of 1872. Never had so many left for that country in so short a time.[99] Dozens of British and American newspapers carried the extraordinary report while the Italian press raised a cry of alarm against the unprecedented desertions.

The May 20, 1872 session of the Italian parliament began with a budgetary discussion, but it abruptly deteriorated into a disagreement about escalating emigration. Concluding a speech about the economy, deputy Guglielmo Tocci broached a topic ignored by Prime Minister Giovanni Lanza, who was among the assembled representatives. Addressing Lanza directly, Tocci exclaimed, "The Italians are leaving, Minister! Emigration is assuming frightening proportions. The people are hit with the salt tax, the grist tax, the lotto, and emigration from places where you need work the most, from where sustenance comes to the cities. What about this fact, honorable minister? Have you studied this very serious social phenomenon that is occurring in Italy? Doesn't it seem worthy of your attention as a statesman?"[100] The deputy's pointed questions drew a caustic retort from the prime minister. Citing an overall increase in population, Lanza tried to argue that Tocci was mistaken. He disparaged the deputy's claim, declaring "this great emigration that he asserts does not exist."[101] This embarrassing pronouncement by Italy's second-in-command sharply contrasted with the burgeoning tide of Italians fleeing the nation.

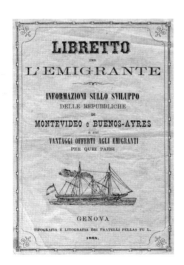

Poster advertising "advantages offered to emigrants" to Montevideo and Buenos Aires. Pellas brothers, Genoa, 1868. *Archivio della Fondazione Paolo Cresci per la storia dell'emigrazione italiana.*

A short article titled "Emigrazione," published on March 10, 1872, in *Il Circondario di Barletta*, reported the egress of the steamship *France* for South America with two hundred Italian emigrants on board. Another story, also called "Emigrazione," appeared in *Il Circondario* on June 23 of that year. The vessel had returned to Italy, but this time it was bearing away a much larger contingent of citizens. The editor solemnly noted the loss to the provincial labor force: "The steamer *France* with 1,100 emigrants left days ago from the port of Naples for South America, among whom over 300 belong to the provinces of Basilicata and Calabria. When we think that those provinces have a very fertile soil and lack arms to cultivate it, we deplore the causes that drive those populations to abandon their own country for another. The government has a duty to study this serious issue."[102]

The *France*, briefly mentioned in the *Circondario* stories, was an integral part of a fleet operated by Compagnia Francese di Marsiglia. Built in 1871 as an emigrant ship, the ocean liner boasted one thousand third-class accommodations.[103] The workhorse of the line, it made several circuits of the Atlantic in 1872, shuttling Italians to South American ports. The vessel was celebrated for a speedy voyage to Brazil in the exuberant account "Notizie Marittime," published on November 21, 1872, in the *Gazzetta della Provincia di Molise*. Undoubtedly, the report of the craft's rapid traverse was intended to whet the appetites of potential ticket buyers. According to the announcement, the *France* arrived ahead of schedule, accomplishing the Atlantic crossing in just twenty days.

A journalist in Naples described the arrival of five hundred peasants from Calabria, Puglia and Basilicata in his September 12, 1872 piece for *Fanfulla*. According to his report, the wayfarers "flocked to the marina lowering their gaze between sky and water, impatient for the steamer that would take them beyond the Atlantic." The author contemplated the phenomenon that drove people from their homes in search of riches in the New World. While reciting the perils associated with their departure, he bemoaned his country's inability to overcome the "national sickness" precipitating the exodus.[104] Another correspondent told his readers of the many emigrants deserting the country and announced his intention to join their egress. "The emigration from Naples is very great; everyone comes here to look for the countryside, and they find the city. I too, do like the others. I came here, arriving last evening, and I leave tonight."[105]

TO ARGENTINA, VENEZUELA AND PERU

The November 9, 1872 issue of *L'Emancipazione* carried the report of a correspondent on the trail of dispirited Genoese workers searching for employment in Buenos Aires. On entering the Argentine seaport, he noted frequent dockings of ships loaded with such fortune seekers. According to the journalist, the men were induced to desert their native land by the "misdirection" of emigration dealers. "The idea is widespread among our compatriots that America is a kind of Golconda mine, where the effort of bending over to collect gold and diamonds is all one need do."[106]

Between 1870 and 1875, the countries of South America received more than three times as many Italian immigrants as the United States, with Argentina receiving the lion's share of exiles. The Argentine Republic vigorously encouraged immigration, as Article 25 of its 1853 constitution confirms: "The Federal Government will encourage European immigration, and it will not restrict, limit or burden with any taxes the entrance into Argentine territory of foreigners who come with the goal of working the land, improving the industries and teach the sciences and the arts." Emigration agents canvassing Europe found a particularly rich hunting ground in the economically distressed Mezzogiorno, where farmers were offered passage, land and tools in the Argentine territories.

Like their northbound brethren, many Italians who traveled to South America endured appalling conditions during transit. On April 22, 1873, a reporter spotlighted the poor treatment of Italian passengers in "Emigrazione," which appeared in the newspaper *L'Italia Centrale*, a paper in Reggio Emilia. Their sufferings were notably similar to those experienced the previous month by Italians aboard the *Erin*. On arrival in Buenos Aires on January 30, 1873, many farmers from the Piedmont region filed complaints with the authorities, having been shipped in conditions "worse than the Negroes of the African coast" had endured. Their contract guaranteed fresh water, bread and meat; instead, they were given salted meat and "chopped biscuit, perhaps left over from previous passengers." According to the account, all third-class passengers were forced to clean the ship. Those refusing the work were "kicked and beaten by the officers on board, and anyone who disagreed was threatened with a knife."[107]

Not all Italians who settled in South America realized the opportunities they were promised, and the Italian press eagerly publicized their difficulties, sometimes using their editorials as warnings to discourage further emigration: "We will never be deterred from advising the working classes of the city and countryside against emigration to America, which is now in vogue. The saddest news about emigrants, etc., comes from there."[108]

In 1874, the industrial world was in the grip of a deep economic recession, the aftermath of the previous year's financial panic. On March 22, 1874, *Fanfulla*'s editor noted the dismal conditions in Buenos Aires, as reported by the Italian consul in that city. He observed "the emigrants who arrived in that port in large numbers aboard the last steamships remain, for the most part, wandering the streets in search of work which they are unlikely to obtain, and therefore they are in the most squalid misery."[109]

Venezuela was another South American destination for Italian migrants. Beginning in 1874, the Venezuelan government instituted a program to encourage immigration, an initiative led by President Antonio Guzmán Blanco. His administration partnered with private groups to recruit foreign laborers, who were enticed with offers of free passage and housing. The incentives attracted almost twenty-four thousand immigrants between 1874 and 1884.[110] Between 1874 and 1888, Italian arrivals to the republic were second only to those from Spain. But in September 1874, Italy's minister of the interior, Girolamo Cantelli, learned about the harsh reception faced by Venezuelan newcomers. It was discovered that country's government allocated the least productive part of its territory to immigrants. But a more serious policy compelled the minister to notify the Vatican and issue a warning to prospective colonists. Cantelli revealed the deceptions hiding in Venezuela's settlement plan and "in what misery the first Italian colonists found themselves" while participating in the project:[111] "A notification published by the *Diario de Avisos* reveals the sad truth of the conditions endured by immigrants to Venezuela, on whom citizenship is imposed, not to obtain for them the rights or advantages of the indigenous people, but to remove them entirely from the protection of the consulates of their country and leave them deprived of the right of complaint."[112]

The following year, the Venezuelan congress formally declared all foreigners within its borders to be citizens of that nation, a ruling protested by the Italian government. The cover of the March 6, 1875 edition of *Gazzetta della Provincia di Molise* carried another urgent message from the authorities in Rome. The *Journal du Havre* published a story claiming the government of Italy endorsed emigration to Venezuela. The administration insisted the assertion was a sham, and the *Gazzetta* declared any such false encouragement constituted "a real trafficking of whites."[113]

Commercial recruiters in league with the Venezuelan government worked zealously to lure emigrants to that country, while Italian newsmen campaigned tirelessly against them. On September 12, 1875, *Il Circondario di Barletta* featured an editorial condemning the practices of the greedy salesmen, stating, "Our royal representative to Venezuela reveals all the deceptions used by speculators associated with that government to stimulate emigration, by promising earnings and resources to settlers, who are instead exposed to bitter disillusionment and the most squalid misery. We will never tire of making these facts public, so that the deluded will change their minds."[114]

On November 29, 1874, Cantelli put out an advisory cautioning Italians against immigrating to another South American nation, this time singling out

Argentina, which was engulfed in a civil war. On March 6, 1875, the editor of the *Gazzetta della Provincia di Molise* described the economic disruption caused by the ongoing conflict, and he counseled his readers to avoid seeking jobs in that South American country.

In the early part of the 1870s, Peru was among the South American republics actively recruiting settlers. With the restoration of peace following an 1872 insurrection, the European Immigration Society of Peru opened an agency in Italy. Eager to attract colonists, the organization offered free transportation and homesteads to Old World emigrants. However, by 1875, the Peruvian economy had deteriorated so badly that its leaders were obliged to end their financial support of the society. Aware that Italian swindlers were operating an illegal emigration racket to that country, Cantelli notified local officials about the scheme. On January 16, 1875, the *Gazzetta della Provincia di Molise* published his warning to anyone seeking their fortune in Peru to avoid being "seduced by the flatteries of the usual speculators."[115]

Despite the shock of so many able-bodied agricultural workers abandoning Italy and the heated condemnations in Parliament surrounding the issue, the freedom to emigrate was never in danger of abrogation. The right was implicit in Article 24 of the Statuto Albertino, the constitution of Piedmont-Sardinia that became the founding document of its successor state, the Kingdom of Italy: "All subjects of the Kingdom are equal before the law, regardless of their rank or title. All shall equally enjoy civil and political rights and shall be eligible to civil and military offices, except as otherwise provided by law."[116] Consequently, the measures available to government amounted to these two: Could shipping lines transporting emigrants be made to follow existing laws? Could the nation improve conditions for the population most at risk of leaving the country? These were the only brakes available to stem the flow.

AN INTERNATIONAL NETWORK
OF EMIGRATION RACKETEERS

The scam artists who defrauded their countrymen based their operations in Italy, but their activities ranged far beyond the Italian border. Agency operatives, stationed along the emigrant route from Italy through Marseilles and Le Havre, handled the dupes at each stage of the trek. On the transit of the *Queen*, an interpreter supervised the victims. And evidence shows the deceptive agents of Turin, Genoa and Naples were familiar with the Italian immigrant neighborhoods of New York City.

On January 3, 1873, the *New York Herald* featured an article titled "The Immigrant Italians; What Caused Them to Leave Sunny Italy for America," which chronicled the voyage of the *Erin*.[117] The story included testimonies from several of the passengers, transcripts of passengers' contracts and a counterfeit transportation certificate. Each ticket buyer received a handful of printed referrals intended to gain instant employment for the bearer. The following day, the *Herald* published two of the seventy introductory letters signed by a representative named Simeone and carried by the defrauded Italians. According to the paper, "They are all addressed to an Italian expressman who lives in Baxter street, and who is represented in Italy to be the comptroller of large public works."[118] Baxter Street is one of the thoroughfares running through Five Points. The expressman named in the letters was Stefano Maggioncada; the 1870 naturalization certificate of a person by this name lists his address as 61 Baxter Street. An 1858 ship manifest recorded the U.S. immigration of a Steffani Maggioncalda; the record indicates he was from Chiavari, located a few miles from Genoa. Not only was Genoa the base of one of the fraudulent shipping companies listed on the November 21, 1872 affidavit but it was also the starting point for many of the bilked Italians on the *Erin*.

THE MEZZOGIORNO TARGETED FOR FRAUD

Keenly aware of the economic privations afflicting the Mezzogiorno, shipping bureaus engaged in fraud used the Italian press to foment interest in emigration from the area. Fourteen Italian newspapers published between August 1, 1872, and January 15, 1873, were examined by the authors. Although ten of the surveyed papers were published in the north, most of the shipping promotions were carried by the four southern journals. In addition, transatlantic steamship advertisements preferentially targeted readers in southern Italy; all four of the southern periodicals featured them.[119]

Several firms with offices in Italy offered passage to the Americas between August 1, 1872, and January 15, 1873. These included the French carrier Compagnia Francese di Marsiglia and Italo-Platense of Genoa, both creditable outfits. Two other Italian syndicates providing overseas conveyance, the National Steam Ship Company and the Pacific

Italian newspapers carrying shipping advertisements from August 1, 1872, to January 15, 1873. *Joe Tucciarone.*

Steam Navigation Company,[120] were thoroughly disreputable. Both were little more than ticket brokers hustling steamship passages at inflated prices. Although both concerns were located in Italy, their names were suspiciously emblazoned in English on their notices in Italian gazettes. The four companies advertised in *Gazzetta della Provincia di Molise*, *Il Circondario di Barletta*, *La Nuova Basilicata* and *Il Risorgimento Lucano*, all of which were published in southern Italy. Clearly, the hustlers were targeting a specific and extremely vulnerable clientele.

A PROTECTIVE SOCIETY FOR EMIGRANTS

By 1876, the hazards and corruption associated with emigration had become so pervasive that they figured prominently in an economic conference held in Milan on January 5. Opinions of the attendees varied widely on the matter. While G. Emilio Cerruti believed the Ligurian region benefited from it, Giovanni Florenzano painted "a very sinister picture of emigration in the Neapolitan provinces."[121] However, all of them agreed that migrants suffered a great deal during and after their journeys. In an effort to reduce the misfortunes endured by expatriates, the meeting's delegates founded the Patronage Society for Emigrants. The editor of *L'Italia Centrale* summarized the conditions that compelled the group to act:

> *Every day we read circulars and instructions from consuls and ministers of every nation who warn the ill-advised and who denounce the false claims circulated by sordid speculators; every day there is the painful spectacle of seeing the trafficking of whites grow while every effort is made to remove that of black slaves. Hundreds of families deceived by emigration agents arrive at the embarkation point with nothing for the crossing of the seas because a wretch to whom they entrusted their goods and money fled, taking all of their belongings; hundreds of families swayed by hearsay embarked in one of our ports only equipped with what is necessary to reach the destination, but there they arrived or were rejected or suffered all sorts of hardships and even death; this is the picture that emigration often presents to us.* [122]

"EVERY MOTHER'S SON OF THEM ABLE"

Back in the United States, the December 12, 1872 *New York Herald* asked its readers, "What is to be done with them?" concerning the flood of Italians swamping the city's port. During the preceding four weeks, nearly two thousand penniless Italians poured through the emigrant depot and spread onto the city's streets. And the deluge was intensifying, much to the dismay of the anxious commissioners at the emigration bureau. Once it was clear that the victims were helpless, the officials began contemplating what to do with them. To fill the immediate needs of food and shelter, the city agreed to harbor them on Ward's Island. Lying in the East River about nine miles from Castle Garden, the island served as a haven for unwanted souls. The insane

"Snow in the City—No Cars Running." *Illustration by Stanley Fox. From* Harper's Weekly, *January 25, 1873, University of Michigan Library* and *HathiTrust Digital Library.*

were sent there, as were hundreds of thousands of bodies removed from Manhattan cemeteries. The island was also the site of the State Emigrant Refuge, where homeless immigrants were housed. The sanctuary became the first American home of the dispossessed Italians.

The unemployment problem was next on the commissioners' agenda. Local assignments provided temporary jobs for some of the men. A large party helped build an earthen dam across the Mill River near Hempstead, the new reservoir providing drinking water for Brooklyn. Two hundred of the newcomers moved a half-million bricks from the upper to the lower part of Manhattan.[123] A far more urgent use for them arose the day after Christmas, when the most powerful blizzard ever recorded buried the city under an eighteen-inch snowfall. The impassable roads brought traffic to a standstill. Desperate for men to clear the snow, the street cleaning department recruited some of the newly arrived Italians, who energetically set about the task, for many their first job since leaving home. The *Herald* reported, "The first honest penny these afflicted fugitives have yet earned in the land of the free came to them yesterday through the means of the beautiful snow. Every

NEW YORK HERALD,
SATURDAY, DECEMBER 28, 1872.

WINTER'S CARNIVAL.

The Grand Assault on the Snow
Blockade in the City.

Embankments Hundreds of Miles
Long Thrown Up.

How the Banditti Shovellers
Did Their Work.

"Winter's Carnival." *From the* New York
Herald, *December 28, 1872, Chronicling
America, Library of Congress.*

mother's son of them able and willing to handle a shovel made as much for half a day's work as he might expect to get for a month's labor in the land of his fathers. It was the grandest sight of shoveling the world ever saw."[124] Shopkeepers on Madison and Fifth competed for the attention of the diggers, some offering fifty cents to have their storefronts cleared.

The next day, residents of the city were happy when the immigrants returned to remove more snow. Bystanders gazed with interest as the column of laborers trudged past. "The saddle colored natives of Italy, over four hundred in number, were scattered along the centre of the great thoroughfare helping to cart away the unsightly mountains of snow banked along either side of the street," reported the *Herald.* "They jabbered incessantly, but they worked well and deserved their wages. The fun these unconscious children of sunny Italy afforded the passers-by was considerable. They rattled away in their own delightful (?) dialect, unheeding the taunts of the small boys crying, 'Tuta-tuta-too!'"[125]

The deep drifts of snow were removed to the satisfaction of thankful pedestrians. This demonstration of their utility gave rise to a change in attitude toward the Italians. The editor of the *New York World* noted the trend and acknowledged the immigrants' efforts, though his compliment was tainted by prejudice: "Walking was a pleasure, and gushing pedestrians relented on the subject of Italian brigands and lazzaroni, and blessed the greasy but useful Neapolitans and Romans."[126]

On January 23, a less severe snowstorm followed and again paralyzed the city. Captain Thomas Thorne, superintendent of the street cleaning department, hired five hundred Italians to shovel the streets. His praise for their performance contained a prophetic overtone: "He says that they are a most excellent class of working men, able-bodied, diligent, faithful, polite, orderly, and exceedingly honest. He has never had to deal with laboring people with whom he has been better satisfied. In his opinion, we are to have a very large immigration from Italy of this class, and he regards their coming as a great benefit to the country."[127] Passersby were amused to see Thorne's "ragged Italians endeavoring to clear away puddles with pick-axes," yet these

Italians clearing snow in New York. *Illustration by Paul Frenzeny. From* Harper's Weekly, *February 1, 1873, University of Michigan Library* and *HathiTrust Digital Library.*

same individuals were grateful for their efforts.[128] Paul Frenzeny captured the scene for *Harper's Weekly*. The snowbound journal's editors commended the exertions of the immigrants and suggested they might start new lives in this country. "We bid them welcome to a land where, under the influence of free schools and enlightened civil and religious liberty, they may find complete emancipation from the chains of ignorance and superstition which their nation has worn so long."[129]

Media coverage of attempts to employ the immigrants varied widely. When a group of them was dispatched to Vermont as woodcutters, a local reporter proclaimed them unsuitable for the work.[130] But the editor of the *New York Sun* received a completely different story. He contacted McNorton and Lawrence, the Vermont firm that hired the men, for an account of their performance: "They are well pleased with the Italians, and say that they all show a willingness to work, and contradict every assertion to the contrary. They add that should the present invoice be a specimen of what are to come, they can find plenty of work at fair pay in that section of the country."[131]

As Italians gained employment in New York, they frequently came into conflict with Irishmen, who were already well-established in the city's public works. In the middle of March 1873, Irish workers digging a sewer near Central Park found they had been replaced by a gang of Italians. The erstwhile workers assembled, intending to attack the new hands, but the police intervened. The contractor in charge of the project had exercised his right to hire whom he pleased, and he chose men who, in his opinion, worked longer hours and did a better job than his former employees. And as

An Irishman warns an Italian immigrant. *Illustration by E.A. Abbey. From* Harper's Weekly, *April 26, 1873, Authors' collection.*

an added bonus for their employer, the Italians accepted a lower wage than the Irish. The displaced workers, among others, were incensed and protested the substitutions. But city council bluntly rejected the appeal:

> *The members of the Board of Assistant Aldermen appear to think that American citizens of Irish birth have a prescriptive right to dig and shovel and trundle the wheelbarrow on the public works of this city. Hence they have met and resolved that the Police Commissioners must give an account of their violation of this right in the employment of certain Italian emigrants to clean our streets. To this the Commissioners reply that they are not "aware of the existence of any law which makes it the duty of individuals or municipalities not to employ an alien."*[132]

THE GIFT OF THE FABBRI

The close of the Civil War and the advent of Reconstruction brought drastic challenges to southern agriculture. Workers bound by slavery to plantations and farms were now free. In addition, many of the over 100,000 Confederate soldiers who died in the conflict were farmhands who never returned to their fields. Virginia was a southern state with too many acres tilled by too few farmers.

On October 31, 1872, the annual meeting of the Virginia Agricultural Society convened in Richmond. General W.F. Lee, president of the organization, recommended a novel solution to the farm labor shortage: the recruitment of immigrants. Governor Gilbert C. Walker promoted the idea in a speech at the Farmer's Convention on November 28 in Petersburg: "We have not one-quarter the population in Virginia that we ought to have. The importance of immigration is generally conceded and it is not necessary for me to say anything on the subject. What we want is honest, industrious, thrifty citizens—who will come and improve and build up our lands."[133] Two days earlier, Walker had received a letter from Bernard Casserly, the superintendent of the commissioners of emigration, announcing the presence of a large number of immigrants at Castle Garden who eagerly sought employment. The general and the governor now had a source for the agrarian manpower they desired. But a construction project in Richmond, which had captured the public's attention, upstaged the demands of the agriculturalists. A group of Casserly's immigrants would

Left: Mary Fabbri, circa 1890. *Right*: Egisto Fabbri, circa 1890. *Emily Randall.*

be enlisted, not as farmers but to help construct a railroad tunnel under Richmond's historic Church Hill district.

In New York, the media sensation surrounding the Italian immigrants generated curiosity among the city's affluent residents. One of these was Mary Kealy Fabbri, the English wife of the influential Italian merchant Egisto Paolo Fabbri. Commenting on her interest in their predicament, the *Charlotte Democrat* heaped contempt on both the aristocrat and the immigrants: "New York philanthropists went wild over them, and the romantic ladies of the metropolis had a lively topic of conversation in the dark eyed, dark haired, olive skinned gentlemen from the classic hills of Abruzzi. It is proposed by a benevolent lady who had been charmed by the brigands to settle them in Virginia, but the Italians don't like Virginia and Virginia won't have the Italians."[134] Despite the closing remark by the *Democrat*'s editor, Mrs. Fabbri financed the immigrants' travel expenses to Virginia, where they would help build the Church Hill tunnel.

On December 16, 1872, the Young Men's Italian Association of New York received a request for two hundred railroad laborers in Virginia. The commissioners of emigration provided the requisite number of individuals for the job, and the Children's Aid Society assisted with the relocation process. This society's mission was finding homes for poor families with children, and some of the men were accompanied by their families. At

Construction of the west portal of the Church Hill tunnel in Richmond, Virginia, 1872.
Chesapeake & Ohio Historical Society.

the urging of his wife, Fabbri donated $1,000 to the commissioners of emigration for the immigrants' travel expenses.[135]

On December 21, 231 Italian immigrants boarded a southbound train of the Old Dominion line. Among them were 18 of the woodcutters who had just returned from Vermont. "Messrs. Brannan & Haggerty, contractors for building the Church Hill tunnel, employed them," the *Richmond Daily Dispatch* reported, "and eighty of them will go to work near Rocketts, while the rest will be employed on the tunnel. They are mostly young and healthy-looking fellows, and will no doubt do a deal of work."[136] This was the first interstate movement of a large number of the disadvantaged immigrants, and their progress was closely watched by the press. They did not disappoint their employers: "The two hundred and thirty Italians who recently arrived here to work on the Chesapeake and Ohio tunnel through Church Hill, are likely to become permanent residents of Richmond, as they like it here and we like them. They are excellent laborers."[137]

Noting the successful experiment in Richmond, a Virginia newsman extolled the employment opportunities in the southern states as options for the unemployed Italian immigrants in New York. "There is room and plenty for those who will work, in our glorious Southern land; they will soon learn our ways, and become part of us, thus giving us political as well as material strength, and settling the vexed question of labor legitimately."[138] Another Virginia editor gave a hopeful assessment of the trial: "The Italians who

East portal of the Church Hill tunnel in Richmond, Virginia. *Photograph by J. I. Kelly, 1938. Chesapeake & Ohio Historical Society.*

have been employed as laborers on the railroad...are said to be sober and industrious men. We hope they will be kindly treated, and their new homes be made comfortable for them."[139] The efforts of the guest workers were so notable that one Richmond businessman was arrested for trying to hire them away from the tunnel worksite.

Fascinated by the saga of the foreign workers, journalists continued to monitor their progress through the spring of 1873. On March 19, a reporter for Richmond's *Daily State Journal* gave the enterprise his unqualified endorsement: "The Italians now employed at the tunnel and on the terminus of the Chesapeake and Ohio railroad are an industrious, frugal, and painstaking class of laborers. In no instance have we learned that they have given anybody trouble. They mind their own business, work well, and promptly pay for what they get. We have room for more of them." A year after their introduction to the South, the newcomers still received a warm welcome in Virginia. One resident offered his plain-spoken appraisal of the guest workers: "They are generally able bodied men, fine looking men—polite, quiet, but good and industrious workmen at lower wages than our people work for, and they are much liked by contractors and the people. They expect to locate permanently in Virginia, and will make good citizens."[140] Completed in December 1873, the four-thousand-foot-long Church Hill passage was one of the longest railroad tunnels in the country. This and other construction projects were temporary, and after their completion, many of the Italians returned to New York. However, some remained in Virginia; for them, America had become home.

GROWING CONTENTION BETWEEN CAPITAL AND LABOR

The Civil War spurred the growth of industry and mining, with workers gaining advantage because of the huge demand for war materials. Not surprisingly, the early 1870s saw increased contention between labor and capital, as rank-and-file workers clamored for improved working conditions, exercising their new power in the attempt to attain them. Among these, the demand for the institution of the eight-hour workday gained traction. At the time, workers often labored ten or more hours daily and some endured a seven-day week. Manufacturers argued that expensive machinery should not stand idle. Abraham Lincoln had seen the growing class of working men

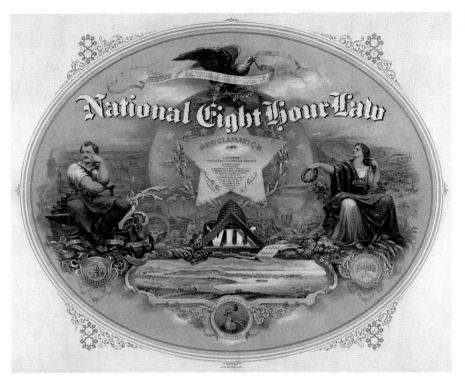

President Grant's National Eight Hour Law, proclaimed in 1869. *Lithograph by Britton & Rey. Prints & Photographs Division, Library of Congress.*

as key to the coalition to preserve the Union and to curtail the growth of slavery. In 1869, Grant's executive order mandating an eight-hour day for federal employees reflected the growing strength of trade unions, as well as a continuation of Lincoln's politics.

The demand for shorter working hours proceeded in fits and starts, accompanied by a series of rancorous strikes in New York's building trades during the spring and summer of 1872. Unyielding managers and recalcitrant employees held firm during the walkouts, and both claimed a measure of success when the disruptions ended in stalemate. This was an era when unions had no legal right to strike. Moreover, the business class considered organized labor to be a constraint on commerce.

As the following year opened, workers threatened another round of uprisings over the prickly issue. Marshaling their constituents, they presented a united front against employers who stubbornly resisted acceptance of the eight-hour shift. More determined than ever to succeed, labor leaders organized a formidable offense for the coming struggle. The *Herald* reported, "The Eight-Hour League, the growing power of the trades unions, which is in fact formed after the fashion of the Council of Ten, and which boasts of being able to bring 80,000 men in this metropolis alone in line against capitalists, has been making preparations quietly for some weeks, in view of the fact that employers have been persistently, since the opening of the Spring business, attempting to make their men work ten hours a day, instead of eight hours, the time adopted as a law by the State of New York."[141]

As in the previous year, the most significant clashes between capital and labor were those that took place in New York City. There the first blow was struck; in early March 1873, a coalition of employers chose to turn back the clock on the gains made by their employees:

> *For some days past a movement has been in progress among the masters to compel the men to return to the old hours of labor, and on last Thursday evening at the quarterly meeting of the Employers' Association, held at Cooper Institute, action was taken in the matter. The meeting was a secret*

Persuading a worker to join a strike. *Illustration by Paul Frenzeny. From* Harper's Weekly, *June 8, 1872, University of Michigan Library* and *HathiTrust Digital Library.*

one, and was presided over by Mr. William Blackstone, President of the Association. During the discussion a resolution to the following effect was offered: "Resolved. That on Monday next we pledge ourselves to use all influence in our power to induce the workingmen in our employ to return to the ten hours system."[142]

ITALIAN IMMIGRANTS AS STRIKEBREAKERS

The die was cast, and shutdowns by disaffected workers soon followed. One of the first was a work stoppage by the employees of the New York Gas Company. With Edison's electric lightbulb still six years in the future, the flickering glow of gas lamps provided the main source of everyday illumination. During the strikes of 1872, a walkout by the gas workers achieved notoriety as "the most formidable calamity with which the city has been threatened."[143] In June of that year, employees struck Manhattan's Metropolitan Gas Works when its owners rejected the eight-hour system. Inexperienced replacements were hired but could not produce enough gas to fill the company's orders. In addition, law enforcement answered management's call to keep belligerent strikers under control. New Yorkers were understandably nervous when gasmen again threatened to walk off the job if operators refused to institute the eight-hour system. On March 21, the Gas-men's Protective Association gathered its members at Constitution Hall to discuss the deadlock. Representatives informed a reporter that the men were resolved to strike and would probably do so on the first of April. The workers' organization planned to shut down the New York Gas Company, the Metropolitan Gas Works and the Manhattan Gas Company. A repeat of the previous year's disruption seemed inevitable, but this time the owners were bringing a secret weapon to the fight. "The reporter was informed that in case of a general strike, Italians would be engaged with a number of men known as 'Scabs.'"[144]

Cornelius Everitt, president of the New York Gas Company, didn't wait for his men to quit. He knew a gas shortage would cause panic, so he moved forward with his own stratagem. While his workers were making plans to strike, he outfitted his shop with bunks and a kitchen. Then, he secretly recruited a group of destitute, unemployed immigrants who were temporarily lodged at Ward's Island. When his men struck on April 5, he replaced them with his new hands: sixty Italians, Swiss and Germans. As the immigrants approached the works, they were attacked by a horde of enraged

THE CAUSE OF THE TROUBLE (AS USUAL)

EFFECT OF THE GASMEN'S STRIKE ON THE EYE OF A FOREIGNER.

An Italian replacement's black eye, presumably inflicted by a striking Irishman. *Illustration by E.A. Abbey. From* Harper's Weekly, *April 26, 1873, authors' collection.*

gasmen. Bearing cuts and bruises, the new hires resolutely entered the plant and began working. Despite their ignorance of the English language and inexperience with the equipment, the foreign workers persevered, and more of them were quickly signed up. The Manhattan Gas Company soon hired its own contingent of Italians from Ward's Island. Within days, it was evident the standoff had failed through the efforts of the immigrant paupers. The *Herald* reported, "The wretched Italians, who had sought on this Continent the exile promised to the humble peasant of the servile powers of Europe, had supplanted the regular and skilled gasmen and had furnished a temporary expedient to 'beat' strikes. Could any other force have triumphed over this strike? It is safe to say no."[145]

The stranded immigrants of Castle Garden now supplied industrialists with the means to bring intractable employees to their knees. The deck had been stacked against the men, and the owners had played a trump card no one had seen coming. The abrupt entry of the refugees into the work pool tipped the scales in favor of the capitalists. According to the *Herald*, "There is one phase of the movement which is worthy of the attention of those studying industrial questions—that the Italians have again been taken from the care of the State, and over one hundred of them placed in an employment where they will be able to earn their own bread and raiment. Ward's Island thus proves a terror to 'strikers.'"[146]

Blindsided and outflanked, four hundred discharged gasmen convened with leaders of the Workingmen's Trade Unions of the State of New York and the International Workingmen's Association. Recognizing the advent of a cheap labor reserve on Ward's Island, the group drafted a proposed law against the employment of foreign workers in the gas industry. The hiring of "pauper Italians" was proclaimed a "direct violation of the pledges to the working classes," and the statute declared that "the action of the commissioners of emigration in importing paupers to our shores to prey on honest labor is a crime which should be punished by dismissal."[147]

In July, the Industrial Congress of the United States convened in Cleveland with the goal of welding the country's independent trade unions into a cooperative entity. The failure of several high-profile strikes in the spring had eroded the bargaining power of American workingmen. The tactic of replacing disgruntled workers with immigrants had escalated to the point that the chairmen of the convention created a special group to address the problem. The Committee on the Importation of Cheap Labor made the following declaration to the assemblage:

> *That as a Congress of Laboring Men, we would welcome to our shores all emigration, whether as skilled workingmen or laborers; that our country is a home for the oppressed of all climes, but that we emphatically protest against the importation of laborers to serve a term of years for a fixed price to compete with the industrial classes of our community, who have made their homes here, pay their proportion of taxes, and use the money they earn for the improvement of the places they reside in; and we demand of the United States Government protection from this unjust competition against our skill and labor, believing that in making this demand we are asking no more than has heretofore been given to capital in the shape of protection.*[148]

On the final day of the conference, the Committee on the Hours of Labor endorsed the adoption of the eight-hour workday. The Committee on Platforms announced a series of resolutions; among them was "the prohibition of the importation of all servile races, the discontinuance of all subsidies granted to mail vessels bringing them to our shores, and the abrogation, or at least the modification, of the Burlingame Treaty."[149] That agreement gave China the status of most favored nation and granted its citizens the right to free immigration to the United States. The protections sought by the committee were finally realized a decade later. The Chinese Exclusion Act of 1882 instituted a ten-year moratorium on the importation of Chinese workmen, who had been replacing American workers at an alarming rate.

The 1873 Industrial Congress also addressed the fragmented state of coal miners' unions. Two months before the Cleveland convention, a five-month stoppage by Ohio miners failed miserably when they were replaced by Italian immigrants from Castle Garden. The bitter defeat prompted an appeal for unity among the nation's miners: "Whereas, the coal-miners of the country, a large and increasing portion of the industry thereof, are being continually imposed upon by and through various corporated monopolies; therefore, be it resolved, that the Industrial Congress earnestly recommend the miners of the country to organize a national association."[150] This they did three months later, when the Miners' National Association was formed in Youngstown, Ohio.

A Serviceable Ethnicity

The recruitment of Italian immigrants as coal miners marks a controversial and turbulent chapter in the history of their integration into American society. Unfortunately, their initial enlistments appear as strikebreakers. This bred hostility and resentment among their American counterparts and at times earned the Italians the name the "Chinese of Europe." Italians were first introduced to the coalfields in March 1873, when one hundred replaced strikers in Coalburg, a mining camp near Youngstown, Ohio. Among the replacements were survivors of the ill-fated crossing of the *Erin*. The Coalburg experiment was so successful that, in May, operators transported one hundred more Italians to replace striking workers in nearby Church Hill, Liberty Township. Jumping out of the frying pan of immigrant deception, the newcomers fell into the fire of a coal war where threats, abuse and murder soon followed. Violence against the blackleg Italians came to a climax at Church Hill, two months after the strikers were forced to end their walkout.

Incensed at their replacement by foreigners, the miners constantly bullied the Italians. Posted notices warned them to leave, and stones were hurled through the windows of their barracks. The simmering cauldron boiled over on July 27, 1873, when two hundred Scottish and Welsh miners, wielding clubs and knives, surrounded a shanty housing eight Italians and one German. Setting fire to the house, the antagonists waited at the

Coal cart from the Church Hill mines in Liberty Township, Trumbull County, Ohio.
Photograph by Ben Lariccia.

windows and doors with weapons ready. The first to escape the flames was the German, who was allowed to leave unharmed on condition that he not summon the police. Alarmed by the escalating situation, he cautioned the crowd against their lawless behavior: "I told the miners if the Italians had done anything wrong to get the constable; the miners replied that they would be constables themselves."[151] Fleeing the inferno, the Italians were viciously attacked by the mob, who inflicted terrible wounds: deep gashes, broken arms and concussions. One victim's leg was so badly mauled that it was later amputated. The last man out of the blazing ruin was twenty-year-old Giovanni Chiesa, who was brutally beaten to the ground and left to die. His coldblooded murder entered the annals as the first documented lynching of an Italian in the United States.

Despite the tragedy at Church Hill, coal operators continued to bring Italian immigrants to the coalfields, especially during strikes. And it was clear that owners had more than one reason for hiring them. In October 1875, John Siney was on trial for conspiracy and unlawful assemblage during a strike in Clearfield, Pennsylvania. President of the Miners' National Association, he encouraged colliers to block the introduction of Italians to the coal banks. He believed the stand-ins were enlisted to boost the owners' intention of destroying the unions. "The importation of Italians and others with no mining experience, and who could not mine coal without a loss, was part of a scheme of the operators to exhaust the funds of the strikers in paying the fares of the new comers back again."[152]

Siney's proclamation echoed the widely held belief that Italians weren't hired for their mining abilities. The Italian peninsula lacks deposits of carboniferous minerals, save for lignite and peat. Instead, the immigrants

"Down Among the Coal Mines." *Illustration by Paul Frenzeny. From* Harper's Weekly, *February 22, 1873, University of Michigan Library* and *HathiTrust Digital Library.*

were pawns in a coal war. It was believed that "in the face of their desire to adjust wages to the condition of the market, foreigners who never saw a coal mine are imported, and for what? To dig coal? No. It is not pretended they can dig. But they propose to learn them. These operators know all the coal they dig for the next six months will cost them more than our miners will work for. This is only an attempt to so utterly demoralize our union men that they will surrender the organization at once and forever."[153]

Nowhere in the country was coal mining more extensive than in Pennsylvania. Throughout the nineteenth century, the state's extraction of the mineral far outstripped the combined outputs of all other states in the Union. In 1875, its aggregate yield of bituminous and anthracite coal was thirty-five million short tons. By 1890, that figure had more than doubled to nearly ninety million short tons.[154] Pennsylvania coal was powering the engines of American industry and its railroads, and an increasingly large army of foreigners was excavating the black diamonds. Pennsylvania coal operators sought cheap foreign laborers, as did shipping companies that profited by bringing them here. "Steam ship companies were interested in selling tickets for fees; and, if statements about jobs and wages in America helped toward that end, they were made. Circulars thrown into their huts and villages by steamship company agents told Italian peasants that they could make from $2.50 to $3.50 a day in the Pennsylvania coal regions."[155]

With such incentives, the business of contracting Europeans to dig in the Pennsylvania shafts flourished. In December 1891, John E. Milholland, chief of the Contract Labor Bureau at the Barge Office, ordered his inspectors to investigate the state's mining facilities. Their inquiry showed what was already well known: a staggering number of immigrants were digging in the pits. "The report of the inspectors shows that the American miner has virtually disappeared. In the places where, less than ten years ago, the majority of the miners were American citizens, there are now not more than ten citizens to every ninety foreigners."[156]

LABOR EXCHANGE FOR THE ITALIAN EMIGRATION

Despite several short-term engagements in the winter of 1873, permanent employment eluded most of the recently arrived Italian immigrants. Recognizing their potential strength, a pair of entrepreneurs established what was, in effect, an Italian-run labor employment service. On July 22, 1873, the

New York Evening Post announced the formation of the Labor Exchange for the Italian Emigration, by the firm of Venchiarutti & Co., located at 49 Franklin Street in New York City. The principals were Domenico Venchiarutti and Angelo Zilio Grandi. According to the article, the goal of the company was the encouragement of Italian immigration to the United States; in fact, the entity's legal name was the Italian Emigration Agency. Venchiarutti said, "We have every facility for supplying railroad contractors, as well as farmers, planters and others requiring collective labor, with reliable, sober and steady hands, accompanied, when so desired, by a foreman and interpreter. Our business is, as yet, as it were, in its infancy; but with the patronage of the all-powerful American press we are confident of developing it to an extent commensurate with the widening fields of Italian immigration and with the ever-increasing American demand for suitable foreign labor." Venchiarutti offered Italian consul general Ferdinando De Luca as a reference; it was a valuable endorsement and a convenient one, since Grandi was De Luca's secretary at the consular office.

A few weeks after its establishment, the agency was contracted to supply fifty Italian laborers every month to the Colonization Society of Port Royal in South Carolina.[157] Port Royal is a small coastal town about fifty-five miles southwest of Charleston. In 1873, it was projected to become the most important commercial hub in the mid-Atlantic region. A proposed railway, the shortest between the Mississippi River and the Atlantic Ocean, was planned to terminate there. Optimists believed the track would eventually reach San Diego, providing a year-round, ice-free corridor. Port Royal's excellent natural harbor was capable of handling large vessels, and steamship companies were considering it as a base for service to New York, Boston and Philadelphia. But stark reality fell far short of grand dreams in November 1873; the community's rail depot was little more than a single-room shanty beside a dilapidated pier, and the hamlet boasted a mere seven houses.[158] Yet tiny Port Royal extended an invitation far and wide to potential settlers in anticipation of boom times to come.

Newspapers from New York to Georgia hailed the plan to settle five hundred Italian families in tiny Almeda, forty miles from Port Royal. De Luca endorsed the idea and predicted its success. A story titled "Italian Immigration," published in the December 18 *Edgefield Advertiser*, reported Grandi's arrival in Charleston; he was on his way to Almeda, near Port Royal, to inspect a newly founded colony of Italians. Seemingly disappointed with it, he voiced his concerns in "The Italian Colony at Almeda," which appeared in the *Port Royal Commercial* on Christmas Day, 1873. He claimed

Port Royal, South Carolina, from a sketch by W.J. Wharington. *From* Frank Leslie's Illustrated Newspaper, *November 15, 1873, Accessible Archives Inc, www.accessible-archives.com.*

the Colonization Society of Port Royal consisted of nothing more than a single office inhabited by a Mr. Papin, the society's sole associate and its reputed president. According to Grandi, twenty-three Italian colonists who came to Almeda did not receive the animals, tools or food promised in an agreement with Papin's operation. This apparent breach of contract prompted Grandi to relocate the pioneers to another plantation ten miles away in Brunson, South Carolina. On the same day, "The Almeda Colony," a news article explaining Papin's version of the mess, appeared in Augusta, Georgia's paper, the *Daily Chronicle and Sentinel.* He claimed Grandi hadn't studied the contract or inspected the site. Papin listed his expenses for the failed endeavor and indicated his firm belief that he had adhered to the terms of the agreement.

The enthusiastic press coverage for this pursuit quickly subsided. In October 1874, ending his partnership with Grandi, Venchiarutti faded from public attention. Grandi[159] returned to Italy, taking a position at the *Banca Popolare* in Vicenza. Their project, the Labor Exchange for the Italian Emigration, seems to have been a short-lived undertaking that ended in failure, or it was possibly a scam. Census records show that in 1880, there were no Italian-born residents in Hampton County, where Almeda and Brunson are located. Consul De Luca represented the interests of Italy's government, including the immigration of its citizens to the United States.

As his secretary, Grandi would have been privy to diplomatic intelligence exchanged between the two nations. And as owner of the labor exchange, just a mile from the Italian Consulate, Grandi stood to benefit from any inside information he obtained from De Luca. The consul's integrity, already questioned by Roberto Prati, was now under scrutiny from another prominent Italian expatriate, Celso Cesare Moreno.

By 1874, the traffic in Italian children forced into street begging had reached the status of a national scandal. That year, Moreno took on the alleged protector of the trade, Consul De Luca. In his work on behalf of the children, Moreno also learned about the various frauds imposed on adult Italians. In an interview for the *New York Herald*, he called attention to the plight of hundreds of Italian adults who had been victimized by supposed promoters of agricultural colonies in various states. He described how they had been persuaded to leave Italy by aggressive ticket sellers who falsely promised them "large grants of fertile land in South Carolina, Vineland, N.J., and elsewhere." Customers who couldn't afford steamship passage were offered cash advances if their mortgaged properties were assigned to "the so-called great and wealthy Land Company," operated by hucksters peddling hopeful visions. "But, alas! Such bright dreams

Port Royal, South Carolina, circa 1861–65. *Prints & Photographs Division, Library of Congress.*

soon disappear. On their arrival here they are under the control of their deceivers, and thrown by them into the streets as organ-grinders, some with a little dancing girl and a monkey."[160]

Moreno's charge of fraud against an unnamed perpetrator coincided with the collapse of Grandi's Almeda scheme. Did his assertions allude to Grandi's muddled venture in South Carolina? The deception revealed by Moreno could explain the total absence of Italian-born residents on the 1880 census records for Almeda and Brunson. Perhaps he was correct—maybe the proposed agricultural colony in South Carolina was a ploy intended to lure unsuspecting Italians to New York.

FREDERICK GUSCETTI'S ITALIAN COOPERATIVE LABORERS

During their first fifteen months in New York, the newly landed Italians made little progress in their effort to join the local workforce. With few notable exceptions, they remained an isolated group of outsiders with no permanent prospects. But in March 1874, the disorganized lot found an opportunity that welded them into a cohesive unit, bound by a common purpose. Their work-for-hire agency was called the Italian Cooperative Laborers, and their enterprising leader was Frederick Guscetti.

Their first foray into the American labor arena ended in disaster. In March, Irish workers digging a railroad tunnel through Bergen Hill, New Jersey, struck for higher wages. Guscetti marched to the worksite, accompanied by several dozen of his cohorts. They were confronted by a larger force of strikers who barred their path and warned them to leave. Standing their ground, the Italians were attacked; Guscetti was beaten to the ground and his men fled. Injured but undeterred, Guscetti decided to formally introduce his services to the citizens of New York City. Within days of the Bergen Hill failure, he submitted a detailed street-cleaning proposal to New York's Assembly Committee on Cities. He proposed to "sweep the city clean and keep it clean" for $8,000 per week, a more cost-effective plan than the current one, which employed a large number of Irishmen. Each of his employees would don matching shirts, hats and badges in order to be clearly identifiable while on the job. The Italians would clear streets blocked by heavy winter storms by melting the accumulated snow with steam engines rather than shoveling it into unsightly mounds. Guscetti said his men were not hourly workers;

they would be paid by the job and would do whatever was necessary to keep their districts clean.[161] Guscetti's proposal attracted the attention of the city's *Commercial Advertiser*, whose editor reviewed the plan with interest. He liked the idea of having a large number of men in readiness for any contingency. The newsman's endorsement of Guscetti's Italian tradesmen included a swipe at the Irishmen who currently performed the work: "They are Italians, and simply propose to apply the Italian system to our necessities; it can hardly work worse than the present Hibernian method. We remember what good service the Italians did last Winter in removing the snow, and we should think this method of utilizing them much more practical than their customary avocations of organ-grinding and rag-picking."[162]

In June, Guscetti's plan was put to the test when his Italian hands replaced striking Irishmen on the streets of New York. The Irish strikers attacked the Italians but were driven away by members of the Harris Light Cavalry, a New York regiment formed during the Civil War by Colonel Mansfield Davies. During a meeting of his troop on June 9, Davies motioned, and the membership unanimously agreed, to form an association "to discountenance strikes, and especially to protect the Italian laborers of the city against the attacks of the Irish laborers."[163]

Shortly after Guscetti set up his organization, Edward Stephens and Arthur Wellington partnered to form the New York Italian Labor Company. Both men were experienced in public works, Stephens having served on New York's Board of Water Commissioners and Wellington operating a civil engineering firm. Like Guscetti, they recognized the underutilized potential of New York's Italian colony: "At first the Italians were disposed to distrust the promises of the company, as they have repeatedly been swindled by spurious labor agents among their own countrymen; but they now, it is said, place entire confidence in the managers, and numerous applications for employment are daily made at their office."[164] By midsummer, the company boasted six hundred workmen and had landed contracts with the New York Central Railroad and the Brookline, Massachusetts waterworks.[165] Still, some contractors were hesitant to employ Italians. When bricklayers in New York City struck in June, Stephens and Wellington offered a cadre of men to replace them at a pay scale below that demanded by the strikers. But the contractors refused the proposition, preferring English-speaking workers instead.

Meanwhile, Guscetti was determined to make a go of it. He broadened the scope of his venture and announced his objectives in a manifesto printed in newspapers across the country:

We claim the right to put such prices upon our labor as may seem to us best. We number twenty-seven hundred artisans and laborers under seventy-two foremen. Having heard that a large number of contracts have been taken at panic prices by builders who cannot proceed with their work because of the existing strikes, we hold ourselves ready to undertake any contract or to furnish necessary force at reasonable rates, guaranteeing that prices agreed upon at our headquarters shall be adhered to during the season or the time the work is done, with good security for the full amount of our contract. We claim to be good and useful members of society, and all we ask is to be allowed to work in peace. [166]

Guscetti further added, "After 18 months trial we have gained the praise of our employers and the good will of all good citizens."[167]

The 2,700 men Guscetti's company comprised corresponds to the number of swindled Italians who arrived in New York eighteen months earlier.[168] This, and his mention of their eighteen-month trial, indicates that his men were the ones who came to the United States in the winter of 1872–73 after being defrauded in Italy. Apparently, they mostly held together as a unit during the first year and a half of their residency in New York.

To one journalist, Guscetti's Italian group represented a new beginning in the integration of Italians into American life. He even suggested they might offer a counterpoint to the unpredictable actions of trade unionists, whose crippling strikes of the previous two years had not been forgotten:

To many this will be a new revelation in the Italian life of America. The children of the lazy sun and sensual moon of Italy, who migrate to the wider fields of America, are generally supposed to be a worthless, vagabondish sort of people, consisting of padrones, musicians, thieves and beggars. The records of New York show the contrary. Of the ninety thousand inmates of the city station houses for the first quarter of 1874, only twenty-seven were Italians, and but a few of this number were members of the Cooperative Association. They are playing an important part at present, and will wield still greater influence in the future in holding at bay the trade union laborers, the very spirit of whose organization breeds discontent in the breasts of its members. [169]

Pro-business editors and profit-minded capitalists embraced Guscetti's plans. But his cost-cutting bids would replace existing employees with cheap laborers, a move certain to put his Italian workingmen in harm's way.

DEADLY REACTION IN PENNSYLVANIA

In September 1874, 1,500 miners struck the coal banks along the Panhandle Railroad near Pittsburgh. William P. Rend was one of the operators whose facility was shut down by the action. Rather than negotiating with his obstinate men, he traveled to New York and signed up a contingent of Guscetti's personnel. Led by Rend and Guscetti, 200 Italians arrived in Pittsburgh on September 23. In addition to picks and shovels, the Italians were given guns.[170] The mostly Irish protesters were infuriated by the arrival of the replacements. Two days later, 50 heavily armed men crept toward the Italian encampment under the cover of darkness. Unaware that a detachment of Guscetti's squad was waiting for them, the assailants fired into shacks occupied by the wives and children of the Italians. When the light from a passing train swept across the attackers, the defenders fired back. With 2 of their number wounded, the raiders retreated, but their determination to rid themselves of the Italians was undiminished. At the nearby Fort Pitt Mines, nine houses were doused with oil and set ablaze.[171] A few days later, a horseman rode along the ranks of the old miners, attempting to recruit 200 of them to "clean out the Italians."[172]

The importation of the immigrants elicited a swift and predictable response from miners' organizations. The indignant editor of the *National Labor Tribune*, the official voice of the colliers, vehemently opposed the importation of the Italians. The publisher declared, "Not a bushel of coal should be dug until every last greasy wretch is sent out of the county. The operators who have imported them should be black-listed, and not a bushel of coal allowed to be taken from their banks for six months after the Italians are expelled."[173]

Charles Armstrong operated several mines in Westmoreland and Allegheny Counties near Pittsburgh, including one near the town of Buena Vista. On October 19, he fired his men without warning and asked Guscetti to supply him with new hands. Guscetti rounded up most of the Italians from the Panhandle team and brought them to Armstrong, who housed them in shanties across the Youghiogheny River from Buena Vista. The Italians arrived with their weapons, much to the dismay of the town's residents. Tensions grew among the townspeople, the discharged miners and the Italians. A month of hostility came to a head on November 29 when a party of Italians who had entered the community searching for a doctor were driven off by armed residents. Two drowned while attempting to cross the stream.[174]

"Miner's War," shootout between striking miners and Italian replacements. *Illustration by Jonathan Love. From* Frank Leslie's Illustrated Newspaper, *October 24, 1874, authors' collection.*

Soon, several hundred men, women and children began marching toward the river separating their community from the Italian encampment. The crowd reached the shore and opened fire, commencing a day-long shootout during which three of Guscetti's men were killed. Late in the afternoon, Guscetti's wife, Annie Brown, left the protection of the barracks and walked boldly into the line of fire, seeking a truce. The shooting instantly stopped, ending the bloodshed.[175] That evening, Armstrong's property was set on fire, and the next day, the Italian miners left the county. The following year, Guscetti and Armstrong, "whose offense consisted in defending their lives," were convicted for participating in a riot.[176] Guscetti's Italian Cooperative Laborers had come to an inglorious end. "The experiment cost the operators $30,000, and Guscetti soon after divided his men between charcoal burning and chicken raising."[177]

THE CONTRACT LABOR SYSTEM

In the middle of the nineteenth century, large numbers of Chinese emigrants were recruited to alleviate a labor shortage in the western United States. The newcomers agreed to work for a predetermined length of time at wages that were generally below the going rate. This arrangement marked the American debut of the contract labor system, a business-friendly procedure that helped propel the rapid development of the country's infrastructure, the key to unparalleled industrial growth.

Escaping economic chaos and famine at home, Chinese emigrants flocked to the United States in the 1850s. In the 1860s, thousands of them were hired directly from China to help build the Transcontinental Railroad. Many Americans were angered when Chinese recruits competed for scarce jobs during the depression of the 1870s. As the United States emerged from the financial slump, business activity expanded and thrifty employers resumed their enlistment of cheap Asian workers. Although welcomed by management, the Chinese were reviled by many who viewed their frugality, race and religion with contempt. "The Chinese Must Go!" headlined many newspaper articles, some favoring expulsion of the foreigners from the country. Responding to the escalating animosity, President Chester A. Arthur signed the Chinese Exclusion Act on May 6, 1882, prohibiting the immigration of Chinese workers. Prompted in part

"The great fear of the period" depicts foreigners devouring Uncle Sam, published by White & Bauer, 1860–69. *Prints & Photographs Division, Library of Congress.*

by racism, it also prevented Chinese settlers already in the country from becoming U.S. citizens.

The regulation was brutally efficient. In 1883, the number of immigrants from China fell 80 percent over the previous year's count, and the rate continued dropping sharply. From 1884 to 1889, an average of just eighty-three Chinese nationals entered the United States each year. Although the torrent had been reduced to a trickle, the closure of the Asian pipeline didn't stop the influx of all foreign labor. Unrestricted Chinese immigration was just one aspect of the much larger problem created by the contract labor system: foreigners were displacing American workers at a disturbing rate. Another group would take the place of the Chinese.

Cheap labor fueled the engines of capitalism in the Gilded Age, and industrialists went to great lengths to obtain the valuable resource. The loss of Chinese labor was offset by increased recruitment of men from other countries. The European marketplace became more appealing and profitable than ever, with Italy continuing to provide a rich supply of workmen. By the early 1880s, imported Italian workers constituted a substantial part of the American labor force. In the popular press, the terms "European coolies" and "padrone coolies" joined other racialized descriptors clearly linking Italians to non-white people. The contract labor system was so lucrative, and the accompanying flood of Italian immigrants so ubiquitous, that a public outcry rose against it.

The *Boston Daily Advertiser* led the charge with its April 10, 1882 tirade titled "The Italian Must Go." The column's writer noted that almost seven thousand Italians entered the Port of New York in the first three months of 1882, a far greater tally than during the same period in the previous year. On this basis, he worriedly predicted that by the close of the year, "twenty-five thousand sons and daughters of Italy may overrun the country." One can only imagine his dismay when he observed that the actual total rose above thirty-two thousand. He suggested the increasing rate could justify "a war against the Italians" like the one currently being waged against Chinese immigrants.

Extreme prejudice colored the writer's perception of the Italians; he described them as "unattractive," "obnoxious," "stupid" and "worthless." In sharp contrast, he portrayed American workers as "hard-handed, honest-hearted toilers." Designating the arrival of immigrants as a "menace to our industrial interests," the writer commended the press of New York for initiating an anti-Italian campaign, just as western newspapers had started the anti-Chinese crusade. The writer ended his rant with a summons to action: "The reasonableness of this projected prohibition and persecution is not to be doubted any more than the sweetness and light of the attacks on the Mongolians. Congress must interfere. Acts must be passed. The anti-Italian movement awaits a leader. Who will stand forth to vindicate American labor?"[178]

President Arthur responded to the growing concern over immigration when he signed the Immigration Act of 1882, the first general immigration law in the nation's history. The statute was tailored to reject undesirable immigrants of the sort flooding the East Coast: criminals, the insane or anyone "likely to become a public charge." It also imposed a fifty-cent duty on every noncitizen arriving at any American seaport. Despite the new restrictions, Europeans continued pouring into the country and replacing native workers in many sectors. Relief could only come with a total ban of the contract labor system.

3.

LEGACY

Ongoing Frauds

In January 1873, the Italian government published a set of rules intended to stop the activities of the predatory shipping agents, yet the fleecing of peasants continued unabated for the rest of that year. U.S. census records show the big uptick in Italian immigration in 1872 was followed by an even bigger rise in 1873. And in their year-end review for that year, the commissioners of emigration reported that the majority of the Italians arriving in New York were almost entirely destitute. By this time, it was clear that the exploitation of poor migrants had become a thriving business. In his 1874 study, *Della emigrazione italiana in America*, Giovanni Florenzano commented on the disgusting activity: "Motivated by self-interest, an immense syndicate of numerous subagents and recruiters spreads out in the countryside to hunt men, just like in Kansas they track down wild beasts. All of these people from various occupations, live speculating and profiteering on the poverty of the unfortunate emigrants. So it is that the gravedigger lives with the cadaver and the crows throw themselves in a swarm onto the putrefying carrion."[179] He noted that the racket, which originated in Naples, spread through the provinces and stretched across the ocean by means of cooperation between the scammers and international steamship firms. According to Florenzano, law enforcement did little to discourage the illicit proceedings. He observed how the acquittal of one of the villainous peddlers emboldened the others. Initially, the government's seemingly tough stance against the inhuman commerce significantly reduced the departures of impoverished peasants. Unfortunately, the regime failed to institute a lasting solution to the problem. After a brief hiatus, the bogus hawkers resumed their trade with renewed vigor.

Frustrated by the expanding operations of dishonest salesmen and the inability, or unwillingness, of government to stop them, Italian journalists frequently commented on the situation. As the emigration crisis deepened, their commentaries acquired an increasingly surreal tone. The essay "L'Emigrazione," appearing in *Il Commercio Savonese* on February 18, 1873, mockingly portrayed America as an "Olympus of inexhaustible wealth and immaculate splendor" composed of "happy and laughing districts of magical fruitfulness."[180] A few days later, a Pisan correspondent wrote, "America is described as a promised land where everyone makes a fortune… there is gold, the wages are very high, the food is cheap, no taxes are paid.… Who wouldn't come to America on these terms?"[181] Italian newspapermen clearly perceived the phenomenon of mass migration in its entirety. They understood that the emergence of con artists was indicative of a much deeper problem: the economic malaise enveloping the nation. For many, prosperity remained elusive, causing many dispossessed farmers and other agricultural workers to desert their homeland. As one correspondent grimly observed, "Emigration is now a necessary evil."[182]

On November 21, 1872, five Italian immigrants swore in an affidavit that they were forced to sail to New York after paying the proportionally higher fare for Buenos Aires. They unanimously attested that Francesco Coppa of Naples was one of the ticket vendors who swindled them to America. Two weeks later, an Italian passenger on the *City of Washington* testified that Coppa defrauded eight hundred Italian emigrants.[183] Two years later, the Steam Navigation Company of Naples announced an expansion of its flourishing South American business. The April 25, 1875 edition of *Gazzetta della Provincia di Molise* enthusiastically supported the venture "so that our emigrants can go to a serious company, which responds to them fully, and does not expose them to the risks of fraud, which so often occur with emigration agents." The bulletin named the company's passenger service representative as one Francesco Coppa of Naples.

Coppa's undisguised appearance in this widely read journal, and the public display of his name and address in subsequent advertisements, speak volumes about the relationship between travel agencies and the Italian government. They appear to verify the claims of contemporary sources that the Italian government allowed unethical ticket brokers to operate unhindered. Whether the purported collusion was rumor or truth, the traffic in creating expatriates was booming.

"In Every Village in Italy"

By the close of 1873, the growing emigration movement had attracted the notice of newsmen beyond the United States and Italy. In December 1873, the *London Tablet* published an account of the trend, which was reprinted in the *Boston Pilot* on December 20. The editor of the *Tablet*, referencing a piece from Genoa's *Il Movimento* newspaper, remarked that six thousand Italians departed for the Americas in the previous six weeks. The *Tablet's* editor noted two factors inducing Italy's diaspora, economic stagnation and an advertising offensive from emigration agencies:

> *In every village in Italy the emigration placards are posted up upon the walls of the streets and within the shops to afford information to the peasantry. A few years ago, these placards were rarely to be seen except in the large cities on the Italian seaboard. But now things are changed. The Italians find the pressure of taxation, and the cruelty of forced service in the army, and the dearness of lodging and food, too much for them to bear. Perhaps also they dislike the organized hostility displayed against their faith. Whatever be the cause, they emigrate. And those who emigrate are precisely the men whose departure is a loss to the country.*[184]

The emigrant scam pulled off by the deceitful shipping agents in 1872 was wildly successful. The disreputable agencies and their greedy subcontractors operated virtually unhindered. Conveniently, the Atlantic Ocean provided a layer of protection from accountability to American protests. The impressive attire of hucksters, their fraudulent circulars and a network of collaborators proved potent in netting backward peasants. The slick formula tricked *contadini* and unemployed farmworkers off village streets and into northern European ports for embarkation to the Americas. It worked so well that it became the modus operandi used by subsequent swindlers for years to come. More than four years after the events in New York, the Italian journal *La Libertà* published a front-page story titled "Emigrazione," which described chronic emigration frauds in Italy. The article listed the characteristics of the deceits, which were identical to those reported in 1872: poor Italians, eking out a bare existence in rural districts, were engaged by brazen operatives who concocted stories of distant lands brimming with fabulous wealth. The peasants were convinced to immigrate to the New World, where they found themselves abandoned, penniless and hungry.[185] Ironically, the issue featured an advertisement for transatlantic service to Rio de Janeiro, Buenos Aires and Montevideo.

Despite the press alarm on both sides of the Atlantic, conditions in Italy continued to drive out the country's citizens. On November 22, 1877, the editor of *L'Italia Centrale* published "L'Emigrazione Italiana," a sorrowful account of the peasants who recently left Italy. He termed it a "mournful topic that must be thoroughly studied in order to find remedies for the painful consequences to our beautiful country." Noting the magnitude of the exodus—one of every forty citizens emigrated between 1872 and 1877—and the false promises inciting people to leave, he wailed, "How many deluded Italians abandon their homeland in search of dreamed-of wealth on foreign shores!"[186]

A Shift in Exploitation

The global recession precipitated by the Panic of 1873 temporarily curbed the steep growth of departures, but by the end of the decade, the rate of those leaving was again accelerating. Members of the Italian parliament insisted on government intervention to stop the hemorrhage from what Deputy Guido Baccelli termed "the bloody wound of emigration."[187] On April 19, 1875, the Italian senate authorized a punitive measure to deter the activity: "Anyone who by trade and for profit induces Italians to emigrate, deceiving them by representing false facts or by giving non-existent news, is deemed guilty of fraud."[188]

Dismayed by the continuing duplicity propelling the exodus, a succession of representatives in the Chamber of Deputies called for the regulation of shipping agents. On December 8, 1876, deputy Andrea Secco asked Prime Minister Giovanni Nicotera what his government was doing about the problem. Nicotera admitted that his predecessors had instituted flawed directives that damaged international commerce while unintentionally facilitating the operations of illicit agencies.[189] On June 7, 1878, proposals authored by Luigi Luzzatti, Marco Minghetti and Giacomo del Giudice were read in the Chamber of Deputies. These placed constraints on the practices of steamship brokers and set forth harsh penalties for noncompliance.[190] But the original bait and switch method of the tricksters was giving way to a more sophisticated recruitment process: the contract labor system was making its Italian debut.

In 1882, the Italian Ministry of Agriculture, Industry and Commerce published a study of emigration for the previous year. Commissioners asked provincial authorities which of the following factors influenced emigration among its residents: poverty, recommendations from local speculators or promotions from employees of overseas shipping companies. An administrator in the province of Campobasso blamed emigration on destitution and opportunistic promoters: "Unfortunately, misery is the principle driver that causes small farmers to abandon their home country, not being able to live off twenty *soldi* in winter and thirty in summer. They find it easy to listen to the advice of the agents of the shipping companies who profit off their ignorance."[191] Similar replies from leaders in other provinces show how widespread the immoral dealings of crooked pitchmen were by 1881. In addition to blaming the exodus on poverty, respondents from the province of Avellino pointed to Naples as the base of the ticket hustlers: "It's indisputable that poverty, more than any other cause, drives the inhabitants of this province to emigrate. But the persuasions of speculators and emigration agents resident in Naples contribute to this, who have in every comune one of their representatives."[192]

The number of Italians coming to the United States more than doubled from 1881 to 1882. Fueling this rapid growth was an evolving form of the deception of the 1870s. In 1872, grifters cheated their victims in Italy and deserted them at French seaports. Ten years later, as American businesses sought cheap foreign laborers, gougers enhanced their operations by copying the global workings of the contract labor system, finding advantage in managing the fate of their victims both before departing Italy and then after arriving in the United States.

The means to emigrate were provided for those unable to afford passage to the New World. However, the arrangement contained certain disadvantages for the itinerants. Foreign workers recruited in this way were usually paid considerably less than their American counterparts. Their obligation to an employer could be lengthy, lasting from six months to several years. And they were told when and where to work. What's worse, the potential for high profits attracted unethical dealers to the trade. These criminals learned they could manipulate the system to their advantage by assuming the role

"Newly Arrived Italian Immigrants." *Illustration by Edward Lagarde. From* Frank Leslie's Illustrated Newspaper, *October 25, 1884, authors' collection.*

of employer in the supply chain. In this corrupt version of the business, the contractor now became the boss, retaining complete control of the immigrants, as well as most of their income. This new version of the swindle was more repugnant than the old; not only were immigrants deceived in their home country, but they also arrived in the United States as de facto slaves. The unscrupulous contractor who managed his luckless consignees in this manner was a padrone.

On August 30, 1884, Harrisburg's *State Journal* reprinted an interview with Henry J. Jackson, superintendent of the immigrant landing depot at Castle Garden. In the article "White Slaves in Gotham; the Italian Padroni and Their Victims," Jackson contended that labor bosses were importing Italian slaves at an alarming rate. "When I say Italian slaves I do not mean merely the children who are brought here to beg and steal, but full-grown men and women." Days earlier he noted the arrival of thirty Italian men whose passage was provided by an unidentified trafficker, to whom each had pledged sixty dollars once employment was found. The dealer stood to make a profit, as steamship tickets were only thirty dollars apiece. The superintendent pitied the poor immigrants, whose ignorance made them easy pawns for such rascals. The *Harrisburg State Journal* reported, "The probability is that these men will be hired out to work upon railroad

Arrival of cheap Italian labor in Ohio's Hocking Valley. *Illustration by J. Keppler. From* Puck, *October 15, 1884, Prints & Photographs Division, Library of Congress.*

construction at very low wages, and that the man who brought them over will receive a bonus for procuring them for the railroad contractor."[193] This deplorable use of immigrants constituted an institution widely known as the padrone system.

In late May 1882, a *New York Tribune* reporter covered the curious arrival of a party of 170 Italians at Castle Garden. The men were under a three-year contract to an Italian national, Signor Carlo Baccari, and were to pay him twenty cents a day from their wages plus the cost of the voyage and provisions. The Italian consul visited the group to assure them that they weren't obligated to fulfill their contract to Baccari. But the immigrants said that they would, indeed, do as they had promised their lord before setting sail to America. Furthermore, they told the reporter that they would wait eight days for Baccari to show up with work assignments. With one voice, they refused what was offered them by the Italian Immigration Aid Society, "work free from all conditions."[194]

Their faith in the padrone's promises was unshakeable. Their allegiance was rooted in the feudal rights and obligations the men and their families had lived under for hundreds of years as serfs on the Baccari estates. Though Italy officially ended feudalism in the 1860s, centuries of paternalism and control of the countryside by titled elites had taught many peasants to put their trust only in the powerful. If survival meant surrendering one's wages and work rights to a padrone, then many of the desperate Italians arriving in New York City saw that as the only way to earn a living in America, where so much was unfamiliar and threatening. Was this inherited lack of freedom and unquestioned loyalty in the "old country" the bridge to the padrone system in the new? Had the money economy that so rocked Italy after unification driven nobles to sell the labor of former serfs?

Outraged by the continuing exploitation of Italian immigrants, Celso Cesare Moreno enlisted sympathetic newsmen to publicize and denounce the evil padrone system. His critics described him as a grandstanding opportunist who flitted from one high-profile venture to another. Yet in this campaign, Moreno appears to have acted on behalf of the oppressed. Besides, he was frustrated by the reappearance of his adversaries of ten years earlier, the padrones who trafficked in children. They now resurfaced in a new guise: overseers of a callous labor system that was exploitive but, curiously, not illegal. Deeply concerned about the growing problem, he set out to stop the abuse of his countrymen. In a letter to the Italian king, he described the detestable methods by which peasants were coaxed to leave the country by immoral labor recruiters. Moreno discussed his agenda with a reporter for the *New York Star*: "I am trying to get the King and people of the upper classes to give proper attention to the abuses which are heaped upon the poor and ignorant class of Italians who are brought to America by the padroni. The padroni are terrible taskmasters. Their slaves are more to be pitied than were the negro slaves in the Southern States before the War of Rebellion." Moreno asserted that many Black slaves had been relatively well fed and housed, while half-starved Italian servants were crammed into filthy quarters. He explained that the peasants, though now on American soil, did not enjoy the freedoms of their adopted homeland. Instead, they were essentially indentured servants, marginalized by their masters to a subculture of fear and ignorance. Moreno described a deplorable incident on a New York City street: "The other day I saw an old woman who was staggering along the street under the weight of a huge bundle which she had upon her back. Near her walked a spruce-looking, well dressed fellow. He was a padrone and she was his slave. I asked him why he required a woman old enough to be his mother to carry such a burden. He replied that he was her master, and he had a right to do with her as he pleased." Moreno's interviewer was shocked by this revelation; what had been the scourge of children was now a curse borne by adults. "Full grown men and women, young and old, are tyrannized over by taskmasters. The poor slaves believe that they have real friends in the taskmasters. The slaves are sent out to beg, pick up rags, grind hand-organs and steal. If they do not get enough money to suit the tyrants they are abused in the worst way."[195]

The journalist for the *Star* was aghast that these atrocities were occurring on the streets of New York. The Italian Consul in New York performed his duties in an office in the heart of the city. Since serving the needs of his countrymen constituted a large responsibility of this assignment, he must have been aware of the maltreatment of poor Italian immigrants in the city. Why didn't De Luca use his diplomatic voice to condemn the practice? "Simply because he is a friend of the padroni. I have endeavored to arouse him in the matter, but he is deaf, dumb and blind to my appeals. He does not wish to interfere with the perquisites of the taskmasters. The padroni's slaves are ragged and hungry, and live in hovels in Mulberry and Crosby streets, while the padroni dress in fine clothing and live on the earnings of their dupes. I do not think I exaggerate when I say that there are nearly one hundred padroni in New York alone, and their slaves are numbered by the thousand."[196] By 1884, over ten thousand Italians had been induced to immigrate by padrones and labored in the United States as virtual slaves.

In 1873, Moreno accused then-consul De Luca of allowing the enslavement of Italian children in New York; he now charged De Luca's successor, Giovanni Raffo, with complicity in the unhindered victimization of Italian adults: "The padroni, if unaided by others, could not carry on their infamous traffic so extensively. They are aided by persons who, with them, grow lazy and fat upon the blood and sweat of the poor slaves. This traffic in human beings began in 1867, when Consul-General De Luca came to this country, and from that time until very lately the Italian Consulate has been the headquarters of the padroni and their accomplices."[197]

"Railroad-Builder of To-day"

Economies of scale in construction and other industries led to the proliferation of Italian work gangs in the 1880s. Food and housing were cheaper for a large group of hands than if supplied to a number of men hired separately. Moreover, managers of Italian workers almost always underbid other contractors when competing for jobs. As a result, teams of Italians were readily employed at trades where sizeable numbers of men were needed. Large crews appeared at public works, iron mills and coal mines, but they were particularly evident on railroad projects where they outcompeted all other groups. This trend was illustrated in "Italians as Railway-Builders. Scenes on the West Shore Road," a report published on October 14, 1882 in *Frank Leslie's Illustrated Newspaper*: "The typical railroad-builder of a few years ago was a newly arrived Irish immigrant, ready to do hard work for moderate pay. Of late there has been a marked change, and the representatives of the Green Isle have been largely supplanted in this work by the sons of Italy. So complete has been the transformation, that the Superintendent of Castle Garden recently remarked, 'The Italian is the railroad-builder of to-day, as the Irishman was a generation ago.'"[198]

According to the column, the construction of the West Shore and Buffalo railroad was accomplished primarily by a force of 1,200 Italian immigrants. The job consisted of blasting and grading a roadbed through the Palisades on the Hudson River's New Jersey shore. The workers resided in a nearby

"Italian Laborers as Railroad-Builders," confrontation. *From* Frank Leslie's Weekly *online database, October 14, 1882, Accessible Archives Inc, www.accessible-archives.com.*

"Italian Laborers as Railroad-Builders," a macaroni feast. *From* Frank Leslie's Weekly *online database, October 14, 1882, Accessible Archives Inc, www.accessible-archives.com.*

encampment with their wives and children. Though crowded into meager dwellings, they retained the customs of their Old-World homes: "The occasional loiterer who may be encountered will very likely wear the air and be clothed in the garb of the typical brigand, and the whole aspect of the colony suggests a veritable bit of Italy itself. The Italians, as a class, prove serviceable workmen, are content to live on meagre fare, and easily endure the hardships inseparable from their life."[199]

An enlarging network of rail lines was essential in stitching together the far-flung cities of the growing, rapidly industrializing nation. Railroad building was an arduous and dangerous enterprise in the nineteenth century. The terrain, desolate and rugged, challenged engineers and work gangs. Prior to 1871, only 45,000 miles of track existed in the United States. By 1900, that figure more than quadrupled to 215,000.[200] Railway projects, such as the construction of the Transcontinental Railroad, were mammoth undertakings that involved not only securing materials but also enlisting manpower. It was necessary for operators to hire large troops of men. The construction boom was made possible by legions of Irish, Chinese, German and Italian immigrants who were generally unskilled menials working for low pay. To facilitate the supply of laborers, contractors often rounded up

Construction gang on the Orange & Alexandria Railroad at Clifton, Virginia, 1863.
Photograph by Andrew J. Russell. Prints & Photographs Division, Library of Congress.

groups of individuals from the Italian countryside, shipping them to New York, where trains waited to take them to jobs in the West. The smooth running of recruitment and transportation to the job site required a labor agent, or boss.

On September 11, 1883, the *Wheeling Register* featured an article, "Italian Slavery: How the Immigrants Are Brought Over Under Long Contracts with Bosses." The piece described the exploitation of immigrants by American railroad contractors. A Pittsburgh foreman, interviewed for the story, revealed that Italian railroad bosses brought many of their countrymen to the States: "These bosses are men who have been here long enough to speak a little English and have acquaintances in the old country."

The interviewee explained that when the railroad needed new hands, the bosses would receive commissions to solicit gangs of workingmen through their overseas contacts. The bosses provided the recruits with paid passage for which they signed three-year contracts that included regular deductions from their paychecks. The paper reported, "The gangs are never permitted to come in contact with other gangs during the three years of the contract, so that the men have little opportunity to learn English, and can have little idea of whether or not they are being cheated. As the bosses get 25 cents a day commission from all the men in their gangs, furnish all the food, at what prices they please, and can generally dictate their own wages, you can see whether it is profitable or not, and you further understand why it is the Italian laborers always work in gangs."[201]

Alfonso Bracco was an Italian railroad boss. Born in Italy, he immigrated in 1872 and settled on Mott Street in the Five Points neighborhood of New

---

NEW-YORK DAILY TRIBUNE, TUESDAY, APRIL 11, 1882.

WANTED.—Work for 100 Italians. AL-
FONZO BRACCO, 239 Mulberry-st., New-York.

NEW-YORK DAILY TRIBUNE, THURSDAY, MAY 29, 1884.

200 ITALIANS want work on the railroad; they understand the work very well'; all good men. ALFONSO BRACCO, 283 Mott-st.

NEW-YORK DAILY TRIBUNE, SUNDAY, JUNE 15, 1884.

ALFONSO BRACCO, 283 Mott-st., supplies the best men for the railroad; any amount of them.

NEW-YORK DAILY TRIBUNE, TUESDAY, MARCH 22, 1887.

ALFONSO BRACCO, cf No. 283 Mott-st., will supply men for the railroad to any number and send them anywhere they get calls for.

NEW-YORK DAILY TRIBUNE, THURSDAY, APRIL 1, 1897.

PONSO BRACCO supplies men for the railroads all over the United States; any amount. 282 Mulberry-st.

Alfonso Bracco want ads, 1882–97. *From the* New York Tribune, *Chronicling America, Library of Congress.*

York City. Municipal directories listed him as a shoemaker, yet his 1884 naturalization certificate showed his occupation to be that of a foreman. The latter profession is attested to by numerous advertisements in the *New York Tribune* by which he brokered hundreds of Italians for railroad work. Apparently, the traffic was very good, as one newspaper report pronounced him a wealthy man. When an 1885 law made the contract labor system illegal, he turned to other pursuits, including saloon keeping, soft drink bottling and politics. Yet he made several bold returns to the business of hawking men to the railroads. In 1887 and 1897, he posted a series of advertisements in the *New York Tribune* seeking railroad jobs for his men. In earlier years, his ads described his hands as Italians; these latter notices did not do so. Perhaps he no longer managed Italians, or maybe he was avoiding scrutiny by the authorities. All we know for certain is that he used the nickname Ponso, perhaps to veil his identity, in his final advertisement, which read, "Ponso Bracco supplies men for the railroads all over the United States; any amount."[202]

An Act to End Contract Labor

On June 19, 1884, lawmakers in the House of Representatives attempted to restrain the freewheeling contract labor system with the passage of H.R. 2550, "An Act to prohibit the importation and migration of foreigners and aliens under contract or agreement to perform labor in the United States, its Territories, and the District of Columbia." The Alien Contract Labor Law, also known as the Foran Act, was approved by the Senate on February 26, 1885. Unfortunately, the authorities lacked the means to enforce its provisions. In addition, labor contractors soon devised ways to circumvent the regulation, and the practice of enlisting foreign laborers continued. Between 1885 and 1887, the number of Italian immigrants streaming into the country nearly quadrupled. As infractions to the law mounted, Congress once again confronted the issue. On July 25, 1888, a select committee of the U.S. House of Representatives met in New York to conduct hearings about alleged violations of the 1885 law. Organized by Congressman Melbourne H. Ford, the task force was known as the Ford Committee.

Passengers, ticket sellers and transport managers gave testimonies. Among those subpoenaed for the hearings was F.W.J. Hurst, manager of the National Steamship Company. Chairman Ford asked him about recruitment practices in Italy. "There have been certain allegations in some of the journals—they don't state what companies—that they send agents about the country telling fabulous stories about the demand for labor in the United States?" Ford's observation shows the procedure employed by the bogus salesmen in 1872 was still in vogue. It was also a pointed reminder that the majority of defrauded Italians in that year were transported on Hurst's vessels. Hurst was then questioned by Morrow, who asked, "You stated a moment ago in one instance, or one or two instances, agents had sold large numbers of

Representative Melbourne H. Ford, circa 1873–90. *Photograph by C.M. Bell. Prints & Photographs Division, Library of Congress.*

tickets on the other side at one time. Were those cases where a person would come and make a trade for the transportation of a large number of persons?" Hurst replied, "That has been done, no doubt." He added that his company made such transactions when it operated ships out of London years earlier. In those days, he said, brokers came to him and offered the deal: "We will give you so many passengers if you will touch Havre this time."[203] Le Havre was the French port where the National Steamship Company boarded the deceived Italians in 1872–73.

Between July 27 and 31, fifteen freshly arrived Italian immigrants were interviewed.[204] All but one had been recruited in violation of the 1885 labor law; Giuseppe Menniti emigrated of his own accord. The rest had succumbed to false promises of abundant work and high wages in the United States. Advertisements posted in villages persuaded some to leave. For those unable to afford passage, dealers on Mulberry Street, in Manhattan's Five Points neighborhood, loaned money to buy steamship vouchers. Agreeing to repay the ticket costs, the travelers were unaware they had been grifted until after disembarking in New York. Though they had sought employment, only six of the fifteen received temporary work while the others found no work at all. Dependent on donations from

"Arrival of Contract Laborers for the Coal Mines." *From* Frank Leslie's Illustrated
Newspaper, *August 11, 1888, Penn State University Libraries* and *HathiTrust Digital Library.*

charities, most wished to return to Italy, including Menniti, who hadn't
earned a penny in America.

Two years later, Charles Foster, secretary of the treasury, ordered an
investigation into the factors driving the massive immigration of Europeans
to the United States. Inspectors Joseph Powderly and Herman J. Schulteis
were dispatched to Italy on a fact-finding mission. They found that
numerous "runners," employees of emigration bureaus, mingled with the
residents and told them wonderful stories about high wages and plentiful
work in America. The inspectors learned of Italians in the United States
who obtained jobs for their countrymen in Italy and sent them prepaid
tickets at twice the usual cost for the trip. It was also revealed that Italian
bankers and hotel keepers in New York fully participated in the illegal
trade. Among them was Carlo Barsotti, owner of the Italian American

Immigrants bound for Pennsylvania's coal mines. *Illustration by William A. Rogers. From* Harper's Weekly, *July 28, 1888, University of Michigan Library* and *HathiTrust Digital Library.*

Bank and *Il Progresso Italo-Americano*, the city's largest foreign-language newspaper. Powderly discovered that prepaid passages were available at grocery stores and coal offices throughout the anthracite coalfields—an arrangement, he believed, that required the cooperation of the steamship companies. Schulteis was startled to learn that some U.S. postmasters sold these tickets, and even more disturbing was his discovery that several American vice-consuls in Europe acted as middlemen for shipping lines.

With their identities concealed, Powderly and Schulteis traveled as far as Naples to investigate obtaining contract laborers. The results of their inquiry indicated as many as fifty workers per day could be had but that contacts on Mulberry Street in Five Points could more easily supply the sought-after workmen.[205]

Carlo Barsotti's Ten Thousand Prepaid Tickets

Clearly, the 1885 Alien Contract Labor Law was a dead letter. In the spring of 1890, a joint session of Congress convened at the Westminster

Hotel in New York City to investigate alleged violations of the statute. The inquiry included witnesses from business, government and the immigrant community who testified about the persistent abuse of the law prohibiting contract labor. The illegal recruitment of Italians entered the record of the hearing. Two Italian witnesses who wished to remain anonymous claimed that Carlo Barsotti openly defied the law when he bought ten thousand prepaid steamship tickets in 1888. As a result of this transaction, Italian immigrants on five ships were illegally transported to the United States. One of the unnamed informants was prepared to give ample evidence of abuse at the Ford Committee hearings, but he never appeared. He claimed that Barsotti had excluded him from the final panel of participants.[206]

During the congressional investigation, Louis M. Montgomery, a special agent of the Treasury Department, was questioned about infringements of the labor law. He explained how extensive the contraventions had become, recounting instances in which Italians were hired by padrones, shippers and even former United States consul Franklin Torrey, who recruited emigrants in Carrara, Italy. Describing the enticement of Italian emigrants by recruiters, Montgomery said, "The El Dorado of America is painted in Florentine colors, and it is found to be often a barren waste."[207]

On April 10, 1890, Samuel Gompers, president of the American Federation of Labor, was invited to speak at the joint session. At one point in the proceedings, Representative Herman Stump said to Gompers: "We ask you to give us information. We have summoned you here as the president of this labor organization. I think it is the desire of the United States to protect the laboring man of the United States, particularly against this contract labor, this pauper labor, and to protect him against the evils which you have mentioned. Now, then, as the president of this labor organization, the American Federation of Labor, we call upon you for this information which you have promised to give us. You will find us in sympathy with your views."[208]

Samuel Gompers, circa 1901–3. *Photograph by C.M. Bell. Prints & Photographs Division, Library of Congress.*

During his thorough response to Stump's request, Gompers said, "I don't want you gentlemen to believe for a moment that I have any prejudice against the Italian. I want to say right here there is no national prejudice that prompts me to say anything against the Italian as an Italian, but I have a good deal to say against the Italian, the Irishman, the Englishman, and any other nationality, if he comes here under contract, to take the labor of men who are already employed in this country, or who are out of employment, and ought to be given an opportunity to work first."[209]

CLEARLY, THE LABOR LEADER was not pleased with the record of the 1885 law that had become a paper tiger.

TOWARD A TIGHTER IMMIGRATION ACT

Less than a year after the conclusion of the investigation, Congress passed the Immigration Act of 1891. President Benjamin Harrison signed the measure into law. Its provisions reinforced the Immigration Act of 1882 by introducing new rules and enhancing the government's authority to regulate the growing inflow. Reiterating a proviso of the 1882 law, it forbade entry to foreigners who were "likely to become public charges." The 1891 act also barred admission to "aliens assisted by others by payment of passage," a direct shot at the contract labor system already outlawed by the ineffectual Alien Contract Labor Law of 1885. These two clauses targeted the importation of destitute immigrants who were widely known as "pauper labor." Sadly, the 1891 act also proved unsuccessful; the flood of poor migrants seemed unstoppable. Bosses found ways to dodge the rules, and the business of contracting alien workers flourished into the twentieth century. The following story, published in the *Youngstown Vindicator* on March 1, 1902, exemplified how widespread and coordinated the contract labor system had become: "The influx of immigrants into the Mahoning and Shenango valleys during the past few weeks has been remarkable. It is claimed that a whole ship load has been dumped in the valley, and that they are put to work by the big companies just as soon as they arrive. The Sharon Steel Co. has arranged to secure a train load on Wednesday. The arrangements were made, it is claimed, by an agent who went to Europe and made a contract with the people before they started."[210]

Sharon, Pennsylvania, the destination of the immigrants in the *Vindicator* story, is located on the Shenango River fifteen miles northeast of Youngstown, Ohio. Sharon lies in the middle of what was once the nation's industrial

"The Peril of American Industries—The Pauper Labor Plague." *From* Frank Leslie's Illustrated Newspaper, *October 6, 1888, Penn State University Libraries* and *HathiTrust Digital Library.*

heartland, yet it is fairly isolated from East Coast ports. After arriving in New York, an immigrant bound for Sharon in 1902 would have boarded a train for Philadelphia, where a winding track would convey the passenger through the Appalachian Mountains to Pittsburgh. A third train would complete the final leg of the journey: a 70-mile run through more than a dozen whistle stops to Sharon. The total distance by rail, the most convenient means of travel at the time, was 470 miles. Sharon's distance from the Eastern Seaboard, and its relative inaccessibility by rail, indicate the degree to which the contract labor system had permeated American society.

CARLO BARSOTTI: EDITOR, BANKER AND LABOR CONTRACTOR

In March 1873, Carlo Barsotti arrived in New York aboard the steamer *Greece*. The young traveler was virtually penniless when he reported to immigration authorities at Castle Garden. His poverty and disembarkation from a National Line vessel both mark Barsotti as a likely victim of emigration sharpers. He became naturalized in 1879 and the following year founded *Il Progresso Italo-Americano* newspaper, destined to become the most widely read Italian-language periodical in the country.

Carlo Barsotti, founder and editor of *Il Progresso Italo-Americano*, America's first daily Italian-language newspaper, circa 1890. *Granger Historical Picture Archive.*

With Italians in the 1870s filling some of the most exploited sectors in the U.S. labor market, the image of the sons of Italy took on a decidedly negative tone. Barsotti attempted to counter this impression by sponsoring the installation of statues to honor his famous countrymen, including ones of Giuseppe Garibaldi in Washington Square, Christopher Columbus on Columbus Circle, Giovanni da Verrazzano in Battery Park and Giuseppe Verdi in Verdi Square. He also led the drive to mount the statue of Dante Alighieri in the park named for the famous poet.

In May 1884, Barsotti founded an employment agency, the New York Italian Labor Company. Its advertisement in the October 4, 1884 *Engineering and Mining Journal* offered "any number of strong laborers, at from 50 to 60 cents a day" and that "the laborers will serve from one to five years without demanding an increase."[211] This raised alarms by the media at a time when Italian immigrants were flooding the American labor scene. Five months later, Congress banned the contract labor system, the heart of Barsotti's venture.

In 1882, Barsotti established the Italian American Bank in New York City. In 1888, King Umberto I bestowed the title of cavaliere on the enterprising Italian immigrant. The famous banker and newspaperman died in 1927 and was buried in an exact replica of Rudolph Valentino's coffin. From poor Pisan immigrant to Gilded Age nouveau riche, Barsotti's contracting of Italian pauper labor had provided the foundation of great personal wealth.

CELSO CESARE MORENO, CHAMPION OF EXPLOITED ITALIAN IMMIGRANTS

Celso Cesare Moreno was born in the Piedmont region of northern Italy in 1830. Although trained in a military academy, a tour of duty in the Crimean War convinced him to forgo the life of a soldier. Returning to Italy, he enrolled at the University of Genoa and graduated with an engineering degree, but he lost interest in that avocation as well. The restless energy that drove him from one undertaking to another became his hallmark. It would lead him to Sumatra, the United States and the Kingdom of Hawaii, where he briefly served as its minister of foreign affairs. Because of his high-profile endeavors, his personal contacts eventually included King Victor Emmanuel II, Emperor Napoleon III and President Ulysses S. Grant.

Unfortunately, Moreno's penchant for concocting foreign schemes may have upstaged his humanitarian achievements. In the late 1860s, he noted the appearance of Italian children wandering the streets of New York City. Dressed in filthy rags, they worked in pairs with one playing an instrument and the other begging for coins. To his horror, Moreno discovered they were the unwilling servants of cruel taskmasters, and to his dismay, he saw that Ferdinando De Luca was doing nothing to stop the inhuman practice occurring right under his consular nose. Moreno urged Hamilton Fish to revoke the exequatur allowing De Luca to perform his consular duties, but the secretary of state refused to do so, claiming the action would damage diplomatic relations between the United States and Italy. Contrary to allegations by Moreno, De Luca insisted he had done everything in his power to suppress the sordid traffic. Yet the assertions were confirmed by a document executed in Viggiano, a community in Basilicata. The small town was a notorious epicenter of child slavery, and peddlers of beggary frequently purchased their human merchandise there. In September 1866, a village father leased his two boys to a padrone for 114 ducats. For three years, the youths would be required to play harp and violin for the contractor, who agreed to clothe and feed them. The document contained his signature and those of two witnesses who stood for the illiterate father. After arriving in New York with the boys in tow, the padrone had the contract approved and notarized, with the signature of "The Royal Italian Consul General, Ferdinando De Luca."[212]

Moreno resolved to stop the heartless treatment of the waifs. In 1871, he contacted Cesare Correnti at the Ministry of Public Instruction in Rome, pressing him to dismiss De Luca as Italian consul. At the end of two

Celso Cesare Moreno. *From the* Hopkinsville Kentuckian, *March 29, 1901, Chronicling America, the Library of Congress.*

years, during which the ministry refrained from acting, Moreno launched his own crusade to rescue the young slaves. On August 25, 1873, the *New York Herald* featured a story about the abused youngsters that included praise for Moreno's efforts on their behalf. Titled "Comprachicos," the article recounted the heartrending story of the children who, kidnapped or sold by their parents, were brought in bondage to America. Once in New York, the captives were parceled out to padrones on Mulberry, Baxter and Crosby Streets in Five Points. The piece named the chief traffickers, the *capi-padroni*, as Giuseppe Argenti, Felice Padulla, Luigi Lapettino, Sansone Nocenzo and Vincenzo Lauletta. They trained the children to play musical instruments and put them on the street to beg. Those failing to bring sufficient earnings to their masters were denied food or beaten. Because of poor nutrition and inadequate hygiene, these children faced a mortality rate of 50 percent. The journal commended Moreno's attempts to free the little ones from servitude.[213]

In 1874, several key members of the U.S. House of Representatives took up Moreno's cause. On June 23, Congress passed a bill that Moreno had promoted outlawing the possession of enslaved Italian children. Not long after, the Italian government awarded Count Luigi Corti and Italian consul

Ferdinando De Luca with the Order of the Crown of Italy. The editor of the *New York Sun* considered the royal accolades an insult to Moreno, pointing out that Corti had refused to have anything to do with the bill.[214] The editor of *La Crónica*, a Spanish-language paper in Los Angeles, said the honor should have gone to Moreno, stating that Corti and De Luca "have been paid for what they should have done for the love of humanity."[215]

After the passage of the bill, Moreno turned his attention to overseas projects, which took him abroad for most of the next decade. Returning to the United States, he was disappointed to find that the exploitation of Italian immigrants was more pervasive than ever. By the middle of the 1880s, thousands of poor Italians of all ages were transported to the United States every year in a state of virtual slavery. He renewed his campaign against their overlords, the padrones, who were binding Italians to labor contracts in violation of the 1885 Alien Contract Labor Law. When Congress began immigration hearings in March 1890, Moreno reminded the lawmakers that, unfortunately, the padrones remained unrestrained in their predations.

By this time, Moreno had singled out Baron Saverio Fava, the Italian minister to the United States, as an accessory to the subjugation of Italian immigrants. In the November 17, 1894 edition of the *Colored American* newspaper, Moreno accused Fava of financially benefiting from the deplorable traffic in Italian slaves. For this, Moreno was indicted for libel the following year. He was found guilty of the offense and jailed for three months. He died of a stroke in Washington in March 1901. Local Italian organizations paid for his interment because, by the end of his life, he had been reduced to penury. Two months after Moreno's death, Fava was recalled to Italy at his own request, an incident that spurred newsmen to revive Moreno's charges. Editorials claimed the padrones received aid from the Italian government and protection from Fava. Moreno had been vindicated but by a U.S. press that had grown virulently anti-Italian.

GIOVANNI MARTINO, "THE SOLE SURVIVOR OF GENERAL CUSTER'S COMMAND"

On January 28, 1852, a newborn baby boy was abandoned at the *proietti domiciliata*, the home for foundlings, in Sala Consilina, Province of Salerno. He was baptized with the name Giovanni Crisostomo Martino. Fourteen years

John Martin (Giovanni Martino), trumpeter for Seventh Cavalry, in uniform. *Photograph by David Francis Barry. Denver Public Library, Western History Collection.*

later, the boy joined the Corpo Volontari Italiani, the Italian Volunteer Corps, under the command of Giuseppe Garibaldi. Young Martino added a musical feature to his budding military career: he was a drummer for the troops.

On March 22, 1873, twenty-one-year-old Martino boarded the steamship *Tyrian* at Naples, bound for the United States. The ship arrived in New York after a thirty-five-day crossing of the stormy Atlantic. Seventy-nine passengers disembarked the vessel, of whom seventy-five were Italian males over age fourteen; the vessel was transporting workingmen, not families. Before crossing the Atlantic, the *Tyrian* briefly docked at Marseilles, Genoa and Naples, seaports used by shipping companies guilty of emigration fraud.

The Panic of 1873 and the onset of the Long Depression made job prospects scarce for the young immigrant. In 1874, Martino enlisted in the U.S. Army under the name John Martin. On June 25, 1876, he was assigned as a bugler in the Seventh Cavalry Regiment of Lieutenant Colonel George Armstrong Custer. At that time, Custer's squadron was in Montana engaging the Lakota, Cheyenne and other Plains Indians in the Great Sioux War of 1876. Prior to approaching a large Indian encampment at the Little Bighorn River, he sent Martin and his troops to request reinforcements. As he galloped through enemy territory, Martin was forced to dodge hostile fire from Indians defending the bluffs. Although wounded by a rifle shot, his horse completed its perilous run. After delivering the message to Captain Frederick Benteen, Martin and his detachment found themselves trapped on a knoll where they fought off a series of Indian attacks until rescued two days later. He was not present at Custer's Last Stand, where nearly four hundred soldiers and Indians died fighting. In later years, newspapers proclaimed Martin as "the sole survivor of General Custer's command."[216]

Martin's last combat assignment occurred during the Spanish-American War. In 1904, age regulations mandated his retirement. After relocating to

Brooklyn, he worked as a ticket taker for the New York subway system and then as a watchman at the Navy Yard until his death in 1922. John Martin's body lies in the veterans plot at Cypress Hill Cemetery in Brooklyn; his gravestone reads:

> *Carried Gen. Custer's Last Message; Battle of Little Big Horn;*
> *June 25, 1876.*

THE ITALIAN SHERLOCK HOLMES

Most of the Italians who arrived in New York in the fall of 1872 were unremarkable individuals. They briefly captured the country's attention as their sad tales were chronicled in the national press, but within a few short weeks, they faded into obscurity. Many would eventually merge without fanfare into American society while others would return to Italy. A notable exception was Giuseppe Petrosino who, at age eleven and in the company of his father, arrived in New York on November 8, 1872. The pair disembarked from the *Denmark* in the first shipload of swindled Italian immigrants. Eleven years after his arrival, he joined the New York Police Department (NYPD). It's somewhat ironic that as a police officer he would hunt down criminals who preyed on the Italian immigrant community. A remarkable sleuth with an innate crime-busting ability, Petrosino solved cases other officers couldn't, and he soon earned the nickname the "Italian Sherlock Holmes." Whenever a violent offense occurred in the Italian neighborhood, the men would say "send for the Dago."

Lieutenant Joseph Petrosino. *March 13, 1909,* New York World-Telegram *and the* Sun *Newspaper Photograph Collection, Library of Congress.*

Joseph, as he was known in America, was one of the first native speakers of Italian in the history of the NYPD. Better yet, he was a master of Italian dialects. The lack of response from the mostly Irish police department had created a law enforcement crisis. Fearing reprisals and Irish gangs, Italians refused to help law officers. Some journalists of the period alleged that Italians were useless in police work. Many criminals, having escaped

"The Spread of the Black Hand." *Illustration by William Krieghoff. From the* Los Angeles Herald, *June 25, 1905, Chronicling America, the Library of Congress.*

justice in Italy and now adopting the terrorist name "Mano Nera," or Black Hand, eluded the police. The poor state of police-community relations had given these and other criminals free rein over New York's Italian community, where they targeted shop owners for extortion and kidnapping. Petrosino understood that if the police were going to succeed in protecting residents in the immigrant enclaves, then the force must treat Italians with respect. Language was critical to building bridges between the two. Taking the crisis seriously, police detective Petrosino convinced the NYPD to create the first squad of Italian-speaking officers. The Black Hand soon found itself on the defensive.

In 1895, Theodore Roosevelt, then-president of the city's board of police commissioners, promoted Petrosino to detective sergeant in charge of the homicide division. Five years later, he infiltrated an Italian-based group of anarchists suspected in the assassination of Italy's King Umberto I. Learning of their plot to assassinate President McKinley, Petrosino informed the Secret Service, but the president ignored the warning. On September 6, 1901, Leon Czolgosz, a Polish American anarchist, shot McKinley at close range while he greeted the public at the Pan-American Exposition in Buffalo; the president died eight days later.

Petrosino was a pioneer in the fight against criminal organizations such as the Black Hand and the Mafia. In 1909, he went to Sicily on a secret mission to gather evidence against Italian mafiosi residing in the United States. Just before he departed, the *New York Herald* published an interview with Theodore Bingham, the police commissioner of New York, who mentioned Petrosino's upcoming assignment to Sicily. Though now vulnerable, Petrosino proceeded with his task. On March 12, 1909, while waiting for an informant at a Palermo rendezvous, he was shot to death by a Mafia assassin. Less than four months later, New York mayor George McClellan removed Bingham from his post. Joseph Petrosino's remains were returned to the United States for interment in Calvary Cemetery in Queens. More than 200,000 people took part in his funeral procession, and the day of his burial was declared an official city holiday so mourners could pay their respects. So ended the celebrated career of the legendary crime fighter. In the end, his adopted city paid him honors rarely bestowed upon an immigrant.

RETURN TO NEW YORK HARBOR

Frédéric Auguste Bartholdi's monumental sculpture *Liberty Enlightening the World* has welcomed immigrants to New York Harbor since 1886. Better known as the Statue of Liberty, she is the personification of Libertas, the Roman goddess of liberty, and a towering symbol of American opportunity. The broken chain at her feet recalls the recent abolition of slavery, an achievement of the Civil War. The pedestal on which she stands bears a plaque inscribed with Emma Lazarus's sonnet "The New Colossus," whose closing verse has offered hope to generations of newcomers:

> *Give me your tired, your poor,*
> *Your huddled masses yearning to breathe free,*
> *The wretched refuse of your teeming shore.*
> *Send these, the homeless, tempest-tost to me,*
> *I lift my lamp beside the golden door!*

In 1872, the statue had not yet been created, nor had Lazarus penned her inspiring composition. In the closing weeks of that year, a multitude of Italian immigrants poured into a nation unprepared to receive them. Preoccupied by the reconstruction of its war-torn country, America's collective conscience wasn't ready to place a greeting at the world's doorstep. The hopeful, weary Italian exiles came ashore facing an uncertain future in a land of promise. As public charges, they evoked pity. Their alien customs, foreign language and Catholic religion were regarded with unease. It seemed unlikely that these strangers would ever gain acceptance into a mainstream American culture founded on British ideas of government and northern European folkways. But their unforeseen arrival proved fortuitous at the dawn of the Gilded Age, an epoch of unsurpassed commercial expansion and capital creation. Mining and manufacturing outputs nearly tripled during the period from the 1870s until about 1900. While the outward trappings of the era were those of great wealth, its inner workings were driven by toiling masses of immigrants, among whom the newly arrived Italians would figure largely. While the introduction of cheap Italian labor was welcomed by industrialists, their massive and relentless entry was a contentious issue throughout the end of the nineteenth century and beyond. The public cry for measures to control the incursion of foreigners brought about the Immigration Act of 1882, the Alien Contract Labor Law of 1885 and the Immigration Act of 1891. None of these, however, slowed the coming of Italians to America's shores.

On the contrary, the pace of Italian immigration rose at breakneck speed. Census records show the figures grew at a roughly exponential rate from the 1870s through the first decade of the twentieth century. In 1896, 68,000 Italians entered the United States. This number exceeded that of every other nation, a distinction the Italians would hold for the next eighteen years. By 1900, the tally reached 100,000; in 1907, it stood at 285,731, the highest one-year total of Italian immigrants. In fact, before that year, no greater annual influx to the United States had ever been recorded from any other country. Between 1901 and 1914, nearly one fourth of all immigrants arriving in the States came from Italy.[217] Other countries experienced this remarkable phenomenon as well; Italians were fleeing their homeland in a mighty exodus. "Between 1880 and 1915, thirteen million Italians emigrated to North and South America, Europe and the Mediterranean Basin, launching the largest emigration from any country in recorded world history."[218]

Large numbers of this historic vanguard disembarked as victims of swindles and, later, of predatory labor contracting. Notwithstanding the dire warnings of the Italian press and the prohibitions issued by the Italian government in 1873, the practice of defrauding Italian emigrants boomed. Immigrant ships disembarked in ever increasing numbers throughout the remainder of the 1870s. When operators began taking advantage of the growing reserve of unemployed men available through the Castle Garden Labor Exchange, Americans increasingly began working shoulder-to-shoulder with Italian immigrants. Conflict was inevitable as the newcomers found themselves thrust into the never-ending struggle

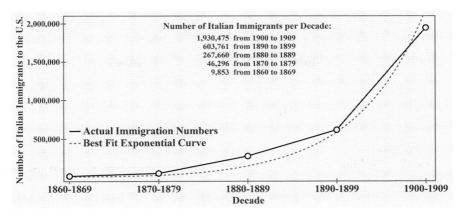

Decadal immigration of Italians to the United States from the 1860s to the 1900s.
Information from National Archives and Records Administration. Joe Tucciarone.

between management and labor. The entry of foreigners into the American workforce created enmity in the old ranks, but employers' demands for cheap working men was insatiable. The contract labor system filled ever-swelling orders for men. Acting as the successor of the swindle, it opened the floodgates to Italian immigration in the 1880s. But the arrangement was both a blessing and a curse. The system supplied capitalists with much-needed muscle to develop the industrial economy, but as aliens replaced American workers, the arrangement aggravated ethnic animosities that would plague Italian settlers for decades.

The surge of jobless Italian immigrants provided capitalists with the means to outmaneuver striking employees during the growing labor movement of the early 1870s. But in their recurring role as blacklegs, Italians learned the hard lesson that walkouts were seldom won by strikers. In 1884, a team of Italian diggers in New York were facing a pay cut that would have caused their American counterparts to strike. Rather than engage in such a risky demonstration, the pragmatic Italians devised an ingenious solution that enabled them to continue working while sending a pointed message to their boss: "The wages of a gang of Italian laborers, near Saratoga, were recently cut down 10 cents a day. Instead of striking they cut an inch off their shovel blades at night. The boss asked what it meant, and one of the men replied, 'Not so much pay, not so much dirt lift; all right, job last the more long; Italian no fool like Irishman; he no strike.'"[219] Nonetheless, Italians eventually joined mine workers and native-born laborers to fill the ranks of organized labor.

Key Events in Italy and the United States

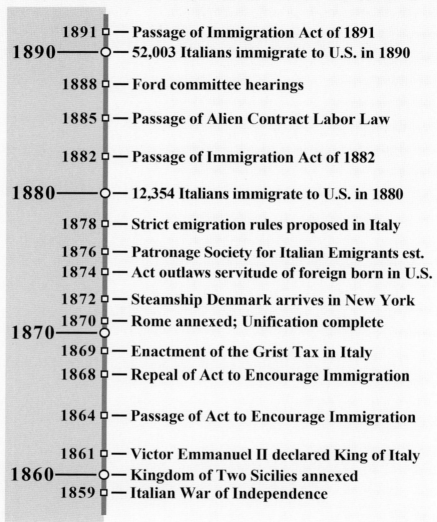

1891 □ — Passage of Immigration Act of 1891
1890———○— 52,003 Italians immigrate to U.S. in 1890

1888 □ — Ford committee hearings

1885 □ — Passage of Alien Contract Labor Law

1882 □ — Passage of Immigration Act of 1882

1880———○— 12,354 Italians immigrate to U.S. in 1880

1878 □ — Strict emigration rules proposed in Italy

1876 □ — Patronage Society for Italian Emigrants est.
1874 □ — Act outlaws servitude of foreign born in U.S.

1872 □ — Steamship Denmark arrives in New York
1870 □ — Rome annexed; Unification complete
1870———○

1869 □ — Enactment of the Grist Tax in Italy

1868 □ — Repeal of Act to Encourage Immigration

1864 □ — Passage of Act to Encourage Immigration

1861 □ — Victor Emmanuel II declared King of Italy
1860———○— Kingdom of Two Sicilies annexed
1859 □ — Italian War of Independence

Timeline of key events in Italy and the United States, 1859–91. *Joe Tucciarone.*

Less than a mile from the Statue of Liberty, on Ellis Island, another plaque speaks of immigrants and the American dream. Some think the words on the panel were spoken by an Italian immigrant for whom reality replaced hope as he soberly assessed his prospects in the New World. Whether this is fact or legend, the remarks are symbolic of the reality faced by a generation of Italians who were lured from their homes by the promise that America was a golden paradise:

> *Well, I came to America because I heard the streets were paved with gold. When I got here, I found out three things: first, the streets weren't paved with gold; second, they weren't paved at all; and third, I was expected to pave them.*

TRANSLATION OF "AVVISO AGLI EMIGRANTI IN AMERICA," *GAZZETTA DELLA PROVINCIA DI MOLISE*, DECEMBER 26, 1872

On December 16, 1872, the Naples journal *La Sentinella* reported the recent emigration fraud uncovered in New York and warned would-be travelers to be cautious when dealing with ticket agents. The newspaper's editor relayed the message to other Italian periodicals, including *Gazzetta della Provincia di Molise*, which reprinted the alert in its December 26, 1872 edition:

In New York, a group of 300 Italian emigrants arrived in November (according to the Times *correspondent), in a most deplorable state. They are Neapolitans for the most part. One of them died as soon as he arrived. It seems they were victims of fraud. They had boarded in Marseilles, where they had been made the most beautiful promises. The Italian minister in Washington was warned of this. After the examination we made, in volume 344 of our newspaper on December 12, of a fraudulent circular, many of which are spread in our provinces to attract emigrants to America, and afterwards the authority of the state police, attended to this with commendable zeal. Our complaints have been received from the offices of these agencies, who are worried about being mixed up with those who are not very moral or very legitimate. Now we must declare that, as was our duty, and in the interest of so many poor people, we thought it well to sound the alarm to other newspapers and warn the authorities and the inhabitants of our province; we need to separate the serious and honest commercial houses, which are dedicated to this industry, from the fictitious and dishonest locusts of their species; discerning one from the other: critical and choice work, which belongs precisely to the prefectural authority, through that of police headquarters.*

"THE IMMIGRANT ITALIANS; WHAT CAUSED THEM TO LEAVE SUNNY ITALY FOR AMERICA," *NEW YORK HERALD*, JANUARY 3, 1873

Yesterday a Herald reporter, accompanied by an interpreter familiar with the *patois* of every district of Italy, visited, for the second time, the recently arrived emigrants from the port of Genoa. These poor people, it seems, have been misunderstood upon all sides. The only truth that has been reached by all the efforts heretofore made is that they are poor and they are miserable. It now turns out that they have been the victims of every phase of misfortune. The representatives of the Italian government here, in their peculiar efforts to defend them, only threw sand in the eyes of honest inquirers. The steamship companies had faults of mismanagement to conceal. The interpreter at Castle Garden was often at fault in his attempts to please all parties, and the result was that the Herald alone came near the truth, from its independent standpoint. It discovered that all were more or less to blame; that certain of the men who arrived had been undoubtedly banditti; that many more had been lazzaroni, and that all of them had been victimized. They were victimized in their own country before they left it; they were victimized at their starting and during every stage of their journey to this country, and they were victimized by their loudest-voiced friends on their arrival.

Some of these men were shepherds, some were small farmers or farm laborers in their own country. They came from the poorest provinces of Italy—from the Abruzzi, from the campagnes about Rome and from Calabria. They all tell a sad story. They were identified with the liberal movement in Italy. They marched and fought with Garibaldi to place Victor Emmanuel upon the throne, and, loving the Pope, they loved liberty more.

Ever since 1860 their taxes, then merely nominal, have increased, gradually swelling up till they engulfed all their scant earnings. Last year they were taxed fifty francs for the house or hovel in which they lived, four francs for each member of the family, four francs for a cow, two francs for a goat and one franc for a sheep. The highest wages they could command were three francs (sixty cents currency) per day. Many who received but two francs were carpenters or stone masons, and were good workmen. They sold everything they had to get to this country, which the agents of the shipping houses of Genoa, Naples and Turin represented as full of everything desirable at a nominal price, while immense fortunes awaited the lucky ones who came to it. Letters of introduction were handed in handfuls to each purchaser of a ticket. They were addressed to an Italian residing in Baxter street, New York, and were supposed to insure instant employment. The following will give some idea of the way in which many of them left Italy:

Statements of the Passengers.

Dominico Manguso, of Armento di Basilicato, in the vicinity of Naples, says: "I am a poor man, and I had a large family. I am about fifty-five years of age. I worked upon a licorice plantation. An agent of Pietro Baero, of Naples, came to my house and said to me that if I came to America I would be some day soon able to return to Italy and live in luxury. The agent gave me a bill of fare, and I read it. I read that I should receive three meals each day. There was fresh meat, fresh bread and potatoes, as well as soups and coffee, included in the bill of fare. So I left my wife and came away. When I got on board the ship I was given only salt meat, and the coffee was not coffee; it was simply a colored beverage given me to drink, and which I had to take, but was without the taste or smell of coffee. The soup, with a slice of salt meat and a potato sometimes raw and sometimes falling to pieces, was our only meal at midday. Some of the passengers fell sick. The doctor came, and in a very short time after he gave them medicine they all died. We all noticed the effect of the medicine and the other sick ones refused to take it. I paid 200f. for my passage from Naples to New York, and came from Havre on the steamship Erin."

Statement of Gennaro Musolino.

"I sailed on board the steamship Erin on December 18. The meals served daily consisted of the following allowance—in the morning one pint of coffee, or, I should say, hot water, and about three ounces of bread. At noon

I got some broth, or hot water with an ounce of rice in it, and three or four potatoes, with a piece of salt meat, the stench of which was unbearable."

Form of Contract for Passage.

The following is a literal translation of the form of contract:

House of Malleggi Marittini, Agency in Naples.
Received from Messrs. Francisco Paslo, Orlando Gabriele, Somiese Antonio, Menadita Felice, Antonio Boccaccio, Michele Angelo and Mestrausi Antonio the sum of 2,290 francs, for No. 6 place of third class (or place convenient in lieu of same), from Naples to New York, with steamship (blank), Captain (blank), which will sail from Havre (blank). Pietro Baero, Agent.

Naples, Nov. 29, 1872.

N.B.—The passengers that have deposited and don't wish to sail lose their deposit.

Some of the passengers made contracts in Havre, and below is appended one of these.

The Havre Certificates.

I, the undersigned, engage to transport conformably to the laws and regulations in the matter, and under all the conditions and indentures of this contract, the persons designated below. Meals are to be at the expense of the agency. Fresh water, cooking, fuel, bunks, care and medicine in case of sickness, light and expenses of hospital, if necessary, are at the cost of the company. The passenger is entitled to the free transportation of 100 kilogrammes or ten cubic feet of baggage for an adult and the half of that for a child. At the request of the passenger his baggage is insured against the risks of the sea for the total sum of *** francs. This contract is valid only for the person herein designated; it can neither be traded, transferred nor altered, and the money when paid will not be reimbursed to the contractor who does not wish to sail, or who fails to do so by his own default. The passenger must conform strictly to all the rules of order and discipline established in conformity to the laws and decrees of emigration. (A copy of the different rules, signed by the captain and approved by the Commissary of Emigration, will be posted up in the cabins of the passengers.)

Appendix II

Extracts from the Law.

The emigrants have the right to remain on board forty-eight hours after their arrival at the port of their destination, unless the ship is obliged to depart again immediately. In case of the voluntary or forced detention of the ship the emigrants are lodged and fed on board at the cost of the ship during its duration, or indemnified for their expenses on shore. In case of shipwreck or of any other accident of the sea which prevents the ship from pursuing her voyage, the agency is held perforce at its expense to the transportation of the emigrant to the place of destination fixed by the contract. In case of the non-fulfillment of the contract the emigrants have the privilege to carry their grievances before the Consuls of France.

TESTIMONIES OF ITALIAN IMMIGRANTS AT THE 1888 FORD COMMITTEE HEARINGS

Excerpt from the testimony of Vincenzo Zurlo:

Q. When did you first make up your mind to come to this country? How long before you sailed? — A. During the winter I made up my mind, hearing the good news of America.

Q. What good news did you hear? — A. The news I got from the placards put up in the village saying that there was plenty of work in America.

Q. What name was signed to these placards, and who put them up? — A. A society in Naples sent them down to be put up on the walls.

Q. Did you pay your passage money? — A. I paid it myself.

Q. How much money did you have before you started? — A. I gave $4 caution money.

Q. What kind of money? — A. Caution money, earnest money, to the man that accompanied us to Naples from the village.

Q. Who was the guide; what was his name? — A. Nicolini Bartoni.

Q. That is the same man that the witness testified about yesterday? — A. Yes, sir.

Q. Did Bartoni make any representations about this country? — A. He said there was plenty of work in America. If we would give him this earnest money he would put us under oath to go to America to earn money.

Q. What office did Bartoni take you to in Naples? — A. The general agency; that is all I know.

Q. Was it a general steam-ship agent? — A. A steam-ship agency.

Q. When you got to New York did you go to work anywhere? — A. Not one day, sir.

Q. How do you live now. — A. I live on charity.

Q. Would you have come here to this country if it had not been for the representations made to you by Bartoni and what you saw on this circular? — A. no, sir.

Excerpt from the testimony of Antonio Angionicola:

Q. How did you get your passage ticket upon the steam-ship? — A. Somebody from here sent the money there for our voyage.

Q. Who received your ticket for you in Italy? — A. A man of another village, not my own, received those tickets.

Q. What was the man's name? — A. This man's name was Olympian.

Q. Who was the man who sent the tickets from here? — A. Gargano.

Q. Where does he live? — A. On Mulberry street; I don't know the number.

Q. Do you know where Gargano got the prepaid tickets that he sent over to you? — A. He bought the tickets of a banker called Barsotti."

Excerpt from the testimony of Giuseppe Granozio:

Q. Who induced you to come to this country? — A. Three people induced me to come here, saying "Go there and you will earn money."

Q. Were these three men scouring the country there and inducing emigration? — A. Yes, sir; looking for men to send off. They were recommending the steamers.

Q. They were runners for transportation companies? — A. Yes, sir.

Q. Did these three men, these steamer runners, have any circulars or advertisements that they distributed around through the villages there? — A. They had bills put on the walls.

Excerpt from the testimony of Gaetano Braccio:

Q. How did you come to think of coming to the United States? — A. A man called Arigo Antonelli told me to go to America and I will find work and good pay.

Q. Was this man Antonelli engaged in procuring others to engage passage to come to America? — A. Yes, sir.

Q. I want to ask you, from your general knowledge of Italy whether this system of inducing men to emigrate to the United States is carried on to a great extent or otherwise? — A. By means of bills and newspapers it is continually carried on, persuading people to emigrate.

Q. Is it carried on to a large extent so that there are hundreds and thousands of them that come here in that manner? — A. Yes, sir; every day.

Excerpt from the testimony of Nicolla Di Alve:

Q. Who furnished you with free passage? — A. A man came from Palmoli called Nicolina Saracina; that is the town where Saracina lives.

Q. For whom were you to work in this country? — A. I came with a letter to America to a man named M. Bernardini, of Mulberry street—No. 54 Mulberry street.

Q. What inducements were held out to you in Italy to come to this country? — A. The inducement held out was $1.50 that Mr. Saracina told me I would earn on this side, and I would thereby be making money for him and myself.

Q. Who was he agent for, or acting for, in inducing these men to come here? — A. This man Saracina kept a store and he was well to do, and he was in correspondence with this Bernardini, of Mulberry street here, and Bernardini instructed him to send men, and he was acting under Bernardini's instructions.

Q. Mr. Saracina is a friend of Mr. Bernardini? — A. Yes, sir; great friends—Godfather they call each other.

Q. Then, if Bernardini lived in Italy, you would call him a cut-throat over there? — A. Yes, sir; just the same.

Excerpt from the testimony of Giuseppe Pedone:

Q. How did you get your transportation or passage across the ocean? — A. From this gentleman from Palmoli.

Q. Who? — A. Nicolini Saracina.

Q. Did you enter into any contract or agreement with Saracina about that ticket? — A. I undertook myself and my wife, in the presence of witnesses, that I was to return 250 francs.

Q. Did Saracina tell you the truth about finding work over here? — A. He told me a story—a lie.

Q. According to your religious principles do you think that you are under obligation and that it is right for you to pay that 250 francs simply because you promised it to Saracina? — A. Yes, sir; I believe having promised it, I have got to return it.[220]

"A REPORT OF THE COMMISSIONERS OF IMMIGRATION UPON THE CAUSES WHICH INCITE IMMIGRATION TO THE UNITED STATES"

Sir: Under authority contained in sundry civil act of March 3, 1891, for the enforcement of alien contract labor laws, I appointed a commission in June last with instructions to investigate in Europe and report to me [Secretary of the Treasury Charles Foster] the facts respecting the importation into the United States of alien contract laborers, and, incidentally, to obtain all accessible information as to the immigration of other classes of aliens whose landing in the United States is prohibited by our laws.[221]

Report of Commissioner Joseph Powderly

In Italy I did not find any circulars or advertisements of any kind, but found that instead each agent and subagent had runners who mingled with the people, giving glowing descriptions of the United States, representing wages as being high, work plenty, Castle Garden as a place where they would be kept and taken care of until they got work; in fact, that it was the business of the officers of Castle Garden to find work for them. The subagents paid runners from one to five francs for each passenger they brought in. On one block in the city of Naples I counted twenty steamship officers, and each one had subagents in all the principal centers of emigration. To illustrate the manner in which emigration is stimulated by the steamship companies, I give my experience on board the steamer *California*, of the Anchor Line, which was to sail from Naples on or about September 29. As her complement of steerage passengers was not full, she did not sail until October 2.

In the meantime, the runners were more active in procuring passengers for the *California*. Saw A.P., keeper of an emigration boarding house, who, as my interpreter informed me, was a "boss" or padrone, endeavoring to secure more passengers for the *California*; saw him talking to and urging intending emigrants to go to the United States, instead of to Brazil as they originally intended. My interpreter, A.D.F., who had been in the employ of the Anchor Line as assistant interpreter, and who had in one year made four trips across the ocean—the last one in May on the steamship *Belgravia*—knew one of the passengers on board of that ship who had been in jail for twenty-five years for murder. The man mentioned had been furnished with a passport to leave the country and was at that time the proprietor of a fruit stand in New York City. My interpreter would not give me his name for fear of consequences to himself in case it became known that he had given such information.

In Naples we were informed that Italian bankers and Italian hotelkeepers in New York are engaged in the contract business. It is principally through their efforts or through the efforts of their correspondents in the emigration centers that so many people are induced to go to the United States. We could not get any direct evidence of the making of contracts, but believe that the contracting is done through these agencies. The following names are those of agents: Banca Tucci, 22 Center street, New York; Carlo Barsotti, general agent steamship line, 2 Center street, New York; B. Bertini, proprietor Hotel Del Campidoglia, 135 Bleecker street, New York, agent for Bank of Tuscany; A. Cuneo, 28 Mulberry street, New York; Banca Italian, 275 Mulberry street, New York; Giuseppe Gallo & Bro., 114 Marion street, New York; Banca D. Garofals, 186 Spring street, New York.

From one of the numerous scribes in the streets of Naples I learned that the Italians were in the habit of writing to their friends in the United States begging of them to take them out of that "miserable country," promising to pay liberally for any money advanced in their behalf. Upon returning to the United States I learned from an Italian steamship agent that he often received such letters, and he knew of several Italians who made it their business to invest their money in that way; that is, by sending prepaid tickets to Italy, bringing over acquaintances, finding work for them, and receiving double the amount expended in bringing them over. This is always paid out of the first money that these men earn.

On returning to the United States I made it my business to trace the prepaid passage business and have discovered that all through the anthracite coal fields the tickets of these steamship companies are for sale in coal offices, retail stores, and corner groceries. This could not be done without the knowledge and consent of the steamship companies; were it otherwise the tickets thus sold would not be honored when presented by the emigrant.[222]

Report of Commissioner Herman J. Schulteis

The prospect for the rich harvest in the Italian emigration of the future has induced the North German Lloyd Steamship Company to open a new line within the last thirty days, to sail from the port of Genoa, in Italy, to the United States, in ships especially fitted up for the traffic. I met persons who represented themselves as their agents, in Sicily, whose business it was to establish subagencies, and travelled with them, together with Commissioner Powderly, to Palermo. They were elated with their success, and anticipated a full share of the trade, as tickets are bought "*en bloc*" on this side and in blank transmitted to the other side, prepaid, to persons who are unable to pay for them until they have earned the money in the United States.

There are about 80 so-called Italian bankers in New York, who have grown prosperous on the interest received on the money advanced for prepaid tickets, and out of the traffic in contract labor. Some of these bankers have been knighted by the King of Italy, and hold their titles to-day, although their former record in courts of justice was very unsavory.

I transmit samples of blank prepaid steerage tickets, which are issued "*en bloc*" to agents, subagents, storekeepers, and even to United States postmasters, by the steamship companies.

Vice-Consul, Gen. King, at Paris, told Commissioners Cross, Powderly, and myself that he had recently noticed large parties of very poor and ragged Italians passing through Paris on their way to Havre and Boulogne; and that neither he nor anybody else could get any information from them or from the steamship companies concerning these emigrants; and he advised us not to consult the steamship companies if we wanted to get information. Some of these emigrants tramp through Switzerland, Belgium, Holland, and Germany to embark from the various ports, such as Antwerp, Amsterdam, Rotterdam, Bremen, and Hamburg.

I interviewed a number of them at Antwerp, and those, who would talk at all, had the same story. They believed that grapes grew wild along our railroads, and that the price of labor was four times as great as in Italy, and that there was a great demand here for their services.

The interpreter whom Commissioner Powderly engaged in Naples (see Report of Commissioner Powderly), and who accompanied us on board the steamer *California*, had been to this country four times since the preceding month of May, in the capacity of an assistant interpreter, paid and graded on the books of the steamship company as a steward, and whose duty it was to instruct the steerage passengers what to say and how to land at Castle Garden. He exhibited his commission as such to Mr. Powderly and myself, and it was signed by a well-known steamship agent in New York City, belonging to the Anchor Line.

Commissioner Powderly and myself represented ourselves as persons who were looking for contract laborers; and while the agents agreed to furnish us with as many as we wanted at the rate of 50 per day, they expressed astonishment that we had taken the trouble to come to Italy for that purpose when it could have been done just as well by their agents in Mulberry street, New York.

I exhibit herewith a circular letter drafted by the chairman of this commission (with the exception of the questions on the last page, which are my own suggestions). I find that out of the hundreds of American consuls in Europe only sixty-seven responded at all. As, unfortunately, a number of our foreign consular representatives, usually the vice-consuls, are very intimately connected with foreign steamship companies, some of them being steamship agents, the unsatisfactory result of these inquiries is not surprising.[223]

"THE BOGUS CIRCULAR"

On November 22, 1872, the *New York Tribune* broke the tragic story of the deceived Italian immigrants who arrived on the steamship *Holland.* The following day, the paper continued its coverage of the affair with "A Remarkable Swindle; The Bogus El Dorado Scheme." One of the fraudulent Italian handbills, printed in Genoa by Pellas & Co., was shown to the *Tribune*'s correspondent, and a translation was included in the article. What follows are the contents of "the bogus circular," as it was called.

Among the States of America, the Republics of Buenos Ayres and Montevideo offer the greatest opportunity for emigrants. The Republics of Central America, on account of the troubles arising from the unhealthy climate, do not offer the advantages common to the better agricultural countries of America. In the United States, except in the Far West, agriculture is not encouraged by the granting of territory to settlers, but in the republics of Buenos Ayres and Montevideo all settlers are given a tract of land. The farmer, besides being surrounded by a European population, finds a pleasant climate much like that of Italy, a fertile soil in which sugar cane and all kinds of produce grow to advantage, large prairies for grazing cattle, forests of excellent lumber for building purposes, fruits of every kind growing wild, and large lakes and rivers. For all sorts of mechanics the demand is very great. The population of the Argentine Confederation is 1,600,000, and of the City of Buenos Ayres 150,000 inhabitants. In the vicinity of that city there are about 60 cities and villages with 300,000 souls. In this region the foreigners represent fully two-fifths of the entire population. The emigration of Italian citizens to the Republic of Buenos Ayres for several years has been as follows:

1858 4,658	1862 6,760	1866 13,950
1859 4,715	1863 10,400	1867 18,646
1860 5,656	1864 11,680	1868 (Genoese)... 16,672
1861 6,300	1865 11,770	1869 22,676

The immigration to Buenos Ayres is, however, as yet in its infancy, for with the 140,000 square leagues of public domain in that republic there are homes for all the lovers of freedom. The wages per month for skilled labor, household and farm servants, in addition to board, clothes, and lodging, in Buenos Ayres, are as follows:

	Francs		Francs		Francs
Farmers	80	Bricklayers	240	Cooks	80 to 100
Gardeners	100 to 120	Shoemakers	300	Sewing girls	70 to 80
Servants, 11 to 15 years	22 to 35	Tailors	360	Carpenters	240
Milliners	80 to 100	Laborers	60 to 80	Blacksmiths	270
Laundry women	70 to 80	Domestics, men or women	60 to 80	Railroad Laborers, in great demand	380

The daily expenses for board and lodging will not exceed 3 to 4 francs, or 90 to 120 francs per month. The prosperity of the Italian emigrants in Buenos Ayres is shown by the fact that they are the largest depositors in the savings banks, in which 20,000,000 francs are kept.[224]

AFFIDAVIT OF NOVEMBER 21, 1872

Felice Carbone, Antonio Grottala, Alfonso Bojano, Michelle Cerello, Fidele Gampolo, being duly sworn, depose and say that they are natives of Italy; that they came as steerage passengers, per steamship Holland, from Havre, arriving at Castle Garden, New York, on the 18th day of November, 1872; that in Italy circulars had been distributed by certain passenger agents throughout the country, stating that a great deal of money was to be made in the United States of America, the Italians residing there remitting considerable amounts of money to their friends, and that wages were as follows: for gardeners, from 100 to 112 francs; laborers, 70 to 80 francs; servants, 60 to 80 francs; cooks, 90 to 100 francs; coachmen, 100 to 120 francs per month, and with board and lodging. That these circulars induced them to come to this country; that those who had cash money paid for their passage, and those who had none executed a certain document, before a notary public, giving as security their real estate for the passage-money advanced, agreeing to pay 15 per cent interest for said amount, and agreeing, if the principal and interest be not repaid in one year from the date, to forfeit the security given, and the same to be disposed of for the benefit of the mortgagee, he being the passenger agent.

Deponents further say that the names of some of these agents are as follows: Francesco Coppa & Co., Naples; Gracomo Fro. Ouejrolo & Co., Genoa; Francesco Palazzi, Naples; Luigi del Tiano & Co., Naples; Rochas Padre & Figleo, Turin; all, as deponents believe, being authorized by the Italian government.

Deponents further say that the rate paid for passage from Italy to New York varied from 250 to 325 francs gold; that some of the deponents had paid their passage direct to Buenos Ayres, South America, but at Havre were forced by employés of the agent, whose name they do not know, to proceed by steamer to New York.

Deponents further say that they are now destitute and without means to provide a living for themselves; and that they would not have come to the United States but for the false statements made by the passage-agents through their circulars, &c., and which circulars deponents believe were distributed in every village and hamlet in Italy.

And further deponents saith not.[225]

"EMIGRANTS' WRONGS; A MOST HEARTLESS SWINDLE," *NEW YORK TRIBUNE*, NOVEMBER 22, 1872

Nearly 300 destitute Italian emigrants have landed at Castle Garden, who have been defrauded of all their money by a band of emigrant robbers. It appears that the emigrant robbers are not alone confined to New York, for the Commissioners of Emigration now have a case under consideration which exceeds in extent any kindred outrage ever perpetrated here.

A bogus colonization society in Havre has been sending its agents throughout Italy, and they have been representing many fabulous advantages offered to colonists in the Republic of Buenos Ayres and in the United States. As the result of a thorough canvass these agents succeeded in collecting at Naples on Oct. 28 nearly 300 emigrants, principally en route for Buenos Ayres. So enraptured were the peasantry adjacent to the towns of Salerno, Benevento, Matera, Capua, Gaeta, and Corvo, that they sold or mortgaged their cottages and small gardens to procure the passage money to a land in which they had been led to expect to find fortunes awaiting their arrival. They parted with their friends in the happiest manner, and those residing in regions apart from the thoroughfares of travel set out with their families on foot, and thus accomplished the entire journey to Naples. Many young men left home for the new world with barely enough money to defray the expenses of the trip, believing that in the unknown land they would have little need for what existed in such marvelous plenty.

They were told that the agents of the great Colonization Society would meet them at Marseilles, at Havre, and at their final destination, to show them every courtesy. They purchased their through tickets for Buenos

Ayres, to the number of 280, paying for them, in many instances, [with] borrowed money which they had secured at usurious rates of interest, and which they hoped to refund after a few weeks' sojourn in the new country of plenty. They sailed from Naples, as before stated, on Oct. 28, and after several days of rough weather on the Mediterranean, reached Marseilles undaunted and more eager than ever to go forward. They were received at this port by men representing themselves as agents of this colonization company, but several say that they believe them to have been the same agents who had sold them their tickets in Naples, and who had followed them by rail. A long and tedious trip through the entire length of France, in an emigrant train, occupied almost as much time as the sea voyage, and materially depleted their already scanty purses. On reaching Havre the emigrants, numbering about 280, were told that it would be many days before a vessel would leave for Buenos Ayres direct, but they were assured that such were the connections of the Society upon this side of the Atlantic that if they would proceed to New-York they would be forwarded thence to their destination free of all expense. Few of the emigrants knowing where Buenos Ayres was situated, and recognizing in the general term of America at least a part of the domain of which they were in search, all were induced to sail in the steamship Holland. They did not realize that they were going thousands of miles out of their course, but began the passage in the steerage with the assurances that they would meet with persons in New-York who would procure them speedy transfer to a southern-bound steamer and rapid dispatch.

On Wednesday they reached this port, and upon landing at Castle Garden presented their letters of introduction and reiterated their confidence in the agents of the Colonization Society. The assurances of the Commissioners of Emigration that no such society was in existence did not entirely open their eyes. They sat down on the benches at Castle Garden to await the arrival of the agents, who, as they said, were coming to take care of them. They were sure of it "because they had been told so." At a late hour last night they were still waiting.

The scene in the large hall of the Garden was a strange one. Gathered around the two large stoves, which heated to redness, gave a cheerful glow to the otherwise dismal quarters, were these wretched Italian emigrants who, stretched upon the floor or seated upon the rude benches, appeared perfectly indifferent as to the future. While this was true of the great majority, several cases were noticed which were extremely sad. Most prominent among the group was an aged father with a large family who clung to him for encouragement, and besought him for some explanation—to tell them why they did not leave such cheerless quarters and seek that beautiful country which they had heard so much about. His agony appeared to be terrible, and he neither shed tears nor offered to his wife or children any words of cheer.

Many are without any baggage, this having been sent from Havre direct to Buenos Ayres by sailing vessel. Friendless and without money, they have apparently determined to remain where they are until something is done for them. They are evidently convinced that they have already done too much in the hope of improving their lot. The Emigration Commissioners have furnished them with provisions during the past two days, but are unable to protect them against the chilliness of the weather. The women and children, who are unaccustomed to weather as severe even as the present, are suffering greatly. Superintendent Casserly of Castle Garden has written to the Italian Ambassador at Washington, has informed the Consul in this city, and has made application to Dr. Ceccarini of the Health Board for the employment of a portion of the men. If no other provision is made for these destitute emigrants they will be sent in a few days to Ward's Island, and be maintained at the expense of the city. The Commissioners are naturally very anxious regarding the result.

STEAMSHIP ADVERTISEMENTS:
AUGUST 1, 1872, THROUGH JANUARY 15, 1873

The shipping agencies engaged in fraud were aware of the economic desperation in the Mezzogiorno. They skillfully aimed their deceptive information about travel to the Americas to appear in southern Italian publications.

Fourteen Italian newspapers printed during the swindle were examined for this study. Seven of the papers, issued in the northern cities of Padua, Pisa, Perugia, Reggio Emilia and Rome, contained no advertisements for transatlantic excursions between August 1, 1872, and January 15, 1873. Only three of the northern Italian newspapers carried shipping promotions during that period. They were the *Gazzetta di Venezia*, Venice's leading periodical; *Il Secolo* of Milan; and Rome's politically savvy sheet, *Fanfulla*. Società Rubattino was the only shipper posting ads in *Fanfulla* at this time, and, except for Bombay, it didn't sail beyond the Mediterranean.

Two French lines with nearly identical names advertised in *Il Secolo*: Compagnia delle Messaggerie Marittime Francesi and Messaggerie Marittime Francesi. The former establishment serviced Near East cities exclusively, while the latter called on ports in the Near East, the Orient and South America.

During the period of the swindle, six steamship companies posted timetables in the *Gazzetta di Venezia*; they were Linea del Giappone, Navigazione a Vapore, Peninsular et Oriental, Compagnia delle Messaggerie Marittime Francesi, La Trinacria and the Allan Line. Five of these included no Western Hemisphere destinations; they sailed exclusively to ports in the Near East and the Orient.

The sixth firm, Britain's Allan Line, announced the inauguration of a route from Bordeaux to Havana and New Orleans in the November 16, 1872 edition of *Gazzetta di Venezia*. Although the operation planned to take customers to an American seaport, it appeared to be an authorized offering by a legitimate business. Unlike the fraudulent bureaus, the Allan Line didn't operate from an Italian location; instead, it directed inquiries to the company's Bordeaux office. In addition, no emigrant deceptions were reported in New Orleans at this time. Besides, the Allan Line ship scheduled to arrive in New Orleans, the *Germany*, never made it across the Atlantic. The vessel was destroyed when it ran aground off the coast of France on December 22.

During this period, *Gazzetta della Provincia di Molise*, *Il Circondario di Barletta*, *La Nuova Basilicata* and *Il Risorgimento Lucano* offered numerous advertisements for passage to the Americas. All four papers were published in southern Italy.

ITALIAN IMMIGRANTS ON THE STEAMSHIP
HOLLAND, 1872–1874

T he steamship *Holland* was the pride of the National Line fleet in the early 1870s. The transatlantic workhorse made fairly regular visits to New York between January 1872 and April 1874, conveying passengers, goods and mail from England. During that period, almost eight thousand immigrants—mostly German, Irish and English—were transported in fifteen Atlantic crossings. Among the travelers were over fifteen hundred from Italy. The accompanying chart displays the percentage of Italians on each voyage.[226]

At first, the *Holland* carried few Italians and bypassed the French seaport of Le Havre. In fact, before November 1872, none of the vessel's five transits embarked there. But on November 18, 1872, 532 Italian emigrants boarded the *Holland* at Le Havre, most falling victim to emigrant grifters operating there. A torrent of American and Italian newspaper reports denounced the trickery, and Italy's prime minister issued a travel advisory on January 18, 1873. As a result, Italian immigration to the United States plummeted; only eight Italians disembarked the *Holland* at its next arrival in New York.

Despite the press sensation, the substantial traffic through Le Havre prompted National Line management to send the *Holland* there on every passage between November 1872 and April 1874. After the falloff in January 1873, every subsequent transit showed a significant and generally increasing volume of Italian immigrants. In addition, the swindlers soon resumed the

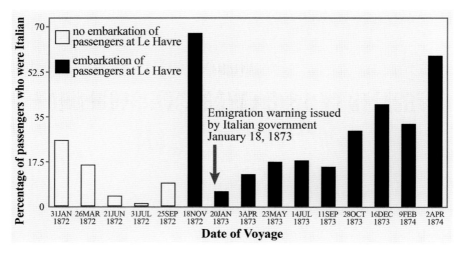

Percentage of Italian immigrants to the United States aboard the steamship *Holland*, January 1872 through April 1874. *Information from National Archives and Records Administration. Joe Tucciarone.*

immoral ticket gouging of their countrymen. Apparently, the fraudsters feared no retribution by local authorities. As suggested by contemporary critics, the Italian government's laissez faire attitude toward emigration seemed to encourage the criminal activity. This lack of effective government regulation of shipping lines contributed to mass immigration.

EXCERPTS OF 1878 EMIGRATION REGULATIONS

The following are some of the emigration strictures proposed by deputies Luzzatti and Minghetti:

The emigrant who has a written or verbal contract with an emigration agent can appeal against him for abuse of contract to the Prefecture or the Royal Consulate whether he is inside or outside the kingdom.

Without distinction of nationality, all individuals or associations who habitually carry out operations for the recruitment or transport of emigrants abroad are considered agents of emigration.

Mayors, state employees, parish priests, and civil and ecclesiastical public officials are prohibited from promoting or curbing emigration in any way.

The emigration agents must have a license granted by the Inspector of emigration issued against a deposit of 3,000 lire annually, under the conditions required by the regulations.

In the application for the license, the emigration agents must declare which are their subordinate agencies, and their clerks or representatives, indicating their names, surnames, and their usual places of residence.

For the execution of contracts with emigrants, the emigration agents are responsible from the day of enrollment until the arrival at the place of destination, without alterations to the contract concluded with the emigrant.

For emigration agents who undertake the transport of emigrants, the provisions of common law for the maritime transport of passengers on sailing or steamships are applicable.

The emigration agents without a license will be punished with imprisonment from one month to one year and with a fine up to 5,000 lire.

The same penalties are subject to mayors, state employees, parochial officers and civil and ecclesiastical public officials for transgression of the prohibition.

Anyone who, as a profession and for profit, represents facts or spreads non-existent news, to induce nationals to emigrate, is guilty of fraud punishable by imprisonment from one to three years, and with a fine up to 5,000 lire.

These are two of the emigration rules proposed by Giacomo Del Giudice:

If, in spite of the special instructions received, the emigration agents deceive the good faith of others with artifices, giving rise to unfounded or exaggerated hopes, the penalties sanctioned by the Criminal Code will be applied in addition to the forfeiture of the license and the loss of bail.

The emigration agents must issue each emigrant with a sheet containing their name, surname and address in the event of complaints. It must also indicate the day fixed for the emigrant's departure, the port of embarkation and the place of arrival.[227]

NOTES

Introduction

1. Louis Gaylord Clark, "The Late William Henry Seward," *New York Evening Post*, November 15, 1872, www.genealogybank.com.
2. The yearly immigration numbers reported by the U.S. Census Bureau do not represent arrivals during calendar years. Instead, the counts generally correspond to entries during fiscal years ending June 30. Exceptions to this rule are 1820–31 and 1844–49, when counts ended on September 30, and 1833–42 and 1851–67, when counts ended on December 31.

Chapter 1

3. U.S. Bureau of the Census, "Chapter C. Migration," *Historical Statistics of the United States: Colonial Times to 1957, A Statistical Abstract Supplement* (Washington, D.C.: Government Printing Office, 1960), 57, www2.census.gov.
4. Ibid., 57.
5. The Piedmontese regime's influence can be seen in the title of united Italy's first king, Victor Emmanuel II, not logically styled "Victor Emmanuel I." This odd nomenclature signified that the post-unification government constituted the continuation of the House of Savoy, a fact that underlined for many the feeling that the Mezzogiorno had been annexed by a foreign power.

6. W.J.C. Moens, "Three Months with Italian Brigands," *Harper's New Monthly Magazine*, June–November 1866, 286, babel.hathitrust.org.

7. *Daily Phoenix*, September 7, 1872, chroniclingamerica.loc.gov.

8. Lucy Riall, *Sicily and the Unification of Italy: Liberal Policy and Local Power, 1859–1866* (Oxford, UK: Clarendon Press, 1998), 57.

9. Robert F. Foerster, "Book IV, Italy Among the Nations; Chapter XXI, The Emigrants—A Study of Motive and Trait," in *Italian Emigration of our Times* (Cambridge, MA: Harvard University Press, 1919), 416.

10. Denis Mack Smith, *The Making of Italy: 1796–1870, Documentary History of Western Civilization* (New York: Walker and Company, 1968), 369.

11. Theresa Finley, Raphael Franck and Noel D. Johnson, "The Effects of Land Redistribution: Evidence from the French Revolution," *SSRN*, 2017, papers.ssrn.com.

12. Ellen Rosenman, "On Enclosure Acts and the Commons," BRANCH: Britain, Representation, and Nineteenth-Century History, edited by Dino Franco Felluga, www.branchcollective.org.

13. "The Norman reunification of the Mezzogiorno, or Southern Italy, revived the custom of pasturing sheep from the upper Abruzzi onto the meadows of the Tavoliere (in Puglia). In close vicinity to the trail of the Abruzzi sheep track, Capracotta found itself in the middle of the highly profitable trade that brings wool from the Kingdom of Naples to Florence," Francesco Di Rienzo, www.lagazzettaitaliana.com.

14. Desmond Seward and Susan Mountgarret, *Old Puglia: A Cultural Companion to South-Eastern Italy* (London: Armchair Traveler, 2006), 14, books.google.com/books?id=21crDwAAQBAJ.

15. Domenico Di Nucci, R' zéngare de *Capracotta*, *Altosannio magazine*, www.altosannio.it.

16. Geoffrey Wawro, *The Austro-Prussian War: Austria's War with Prussia and Italy in 1866* (Cambridge, UK: Cambridge University Press, 1997), 49.

17. Denis Mack Smith, *Modern Italy: A Political History* (Ann Arbor: University of Michigan Press, 1997), 80.

18. William A. Douglass, *Emigration in a Southern Italian Town* (New Brunswick, NJ: Rutgers University Press, 1984), 66.

19. Giogio Brosio, "Coercion and Equity with Centralization of Government: How the Unification of Italy Impacted the Southern Regions," *Public Choice* 177, (2018): 235–64, ideas.repec.org.

20. Smith, *Modern Italy*, 98.

21. "The Love-Hate Relationship of Venice with Water," Venice Insider, 2016, www.theveniceinsider.com.

22. "Studj sull'emigrazione dei contadini di Lombardia," *Annali Universali di Statistica, Giugno 1868* 34, no. 102 (1854–71), 240–42, www. internetculturale.it.

23. Frank M. Snowden, *The Conquest of Malaria: Italy, 1900–1962* (New Haven, CT: Yale University Press, 2006), 30.

24. Smith, *Modern Italy*, 218.

25. Robert F. Foerster, *Italian Emigration of our Times* (Cambridge, MA: Harvard University Press, 1924), 58.

26. Snowden, *Conquest of Malaria*, 20.

27. "Bilancio e finanza pubblica" di Vera Zamagni, in "L'Unificazione," *Enciclopedia Treccani*, 2011, www.treccani.it.

28. "Total Fertility Rate in Italy from 1850 to 2020," Statista, www.statista.com.

29. Douglass, *Emigration in a South Italian Town*, 9, 67.

30. Shepard B. Clough and Carlo Livi, "Economic Growth in Italy: An Analysis of the Uneven Development of North and South," *Journal of Economic History* 16, no. 3 (Cambridge, MA: Cambridge University Press, 1956): 342–43, www.jstor.org.

31. Lo sciopero del 1877: Tessitori e 'beduini,' www.archivitessili.biella.it.

32. Neil Thomas Proto, *Fearless: A. Bartlett Giamatti and the Battle for Fairness in America* (Albany: State University of New York Press, 2020), 17, books. google.com.

33. Clough and Livi, "Economic Growth in Italy," 348.

34. Tomasso Astarita, *Between Salt War and Holy Water: A History of Southern Italy* (New York: W.W. Norton, 2005), 287.

35. Richard Sylla and Gianni Toniolo, *Patterns of European Industrialization: The Nineteenth Century* (London: Routledge, 1992), 201.

36. Warsan Shire, "Home," Facing History and Ourselves, 2019, www. facinghistory.org.

37. "Philadelphia, January 21. Further Intelligence by the Latest Arrivals from Europe," *Gazette of the United States*, January 21, 1792, chroniclingamerica. loc.gov.

38. *Independent Gazette; or the New-York Journal Revived*, January 24, 1784, www. genealogybank.com.

39. *Washington Evening Star*, April 17, 1857, chroniclingamerica.loc.gov.

40. "Lodgings; Night Life in the Slums," *New York Tribune*, May 5, 1871, chroniclingamerica.loc.gov.

41. "A Summer Evening Scene at Five Points," *Frank Leslie's Illustrated Newspaper*, August 16, 1873, www.accessible-archives.com.

42. *Padrone* is the Italian word for master or boss; the Italian plural is *padroni*, in English, *padrones*.
43. *American Emigrant Company* (New York: Office of the Iron Age, 1865), 1, books.google.com.
44. "Foreign Emigration," *Congressional Series of United States Public Documents* (Washington, D.C.: U.S. Government Printing Office, 1864), 1, books. google.com.
45. Ibid., 1–2.
46. "An Act to Encourage Immigration," Library of Congress, www.loc.gov.

Chapter 2

47. See Appendix VI for the full text of the affidavit.
48. "Landing of Foreign Convicts on Our Shores," *Congressional Series of United States Public Documents* vol. 1614 (Washington, D.C.: U.S. Government Printing Office, 1874), 49, babel.hathitrust.org.
49. See Appendix VII for the full text of the article.
50. "Emigrants' Wrongs; A Most Heartless Swindle," *New York Tribune*, November 22, 1872, chroniclingamerica.loc.gov.
51. Ibid.
52. "A Remarkable Swindle; The Bogus El Dorado Scheme," *New York Tribune*, November 23, 1872, chroniclingamerica.loc.gov.
53. "Italian Brigands in New York," *New York World*, December 12, 1872, newspaperarchive.com.
54. "Landing of Foreign Convicts," 47–48.
55. "Les Brigands," *New York Herald*, December 13, 1872, chroniclingamerica. loc.gov.
56. "The Brigands; Something More of the Italian Irruption," *New York Herald*, December 14, 1872, chroniclingamerica.loc.gov.
57. In 1875, a Roman newspaper editor scorned the characterization of all Italians as *banditti* by Americans who, "when they want to represent the 'Italian type,' depict him as a tramp, with a pointed hat on his head, and a kitchen knife hidden under a majestic robe." *Fanfulla*, January 13, 1875, digitale.bnc.roma.sbn.it.
58. "The Brigands; Something More."
59. "Italian Immigrants," *New York Herald*, December 16, 1872, chroniclingamerica.loc.gov.

60. "New York," *Chicago Daily Tribune*, December 19, 1872, chroniclingamerica.loc.gov.
61. "The Italian Emigrants," *New York Herald*, December 12, 1872, chroniclingamerica.loc.gov.
62. "Italian Emigrants," December 16, 1872.
63. Ibid.
64. "The Italians; More of the Emigration Machinery," *New York Herald*, January 4, 1873, chroniclingamerica.loc.gov.
65. Ibid.
66. Ibid.
67. "Testimonial," *New York Herald*, November 2, 1872, chroniclingamerica.loc.gov.
68. Joseph P. McDonnell, "The Ocean Steerage Abuses," *New York Herald*, March 8, 1873, chroniclingamerica.loc.gov.
69. Joseph P. McDonnell, "Ocean Steerage Abuses," *New York Herald*, February 21, 1873, chroniclingamerica.loc.gov.
70. Herbert George Gutman, *Power and Culture: Essays on the American Working Class* (New York: New Press, 1987), 100.
71. "Italy," *New York Herald*, January 21, 1873, chroniclingamerica.loc.gov.
72. Baero was named as an agent in the testimonies of several *Erin* passengers. See Appendix II.
73. See Appendix I for an excerpt of the article.
74. "Emigranti Italiani Negli Stati-Uniti," *Il Circondario di Barletta*, January 12, 1873, www.internetculturale.it.
75. Office of the Historian, United States Department of State, *Papers Relating to the Foreign Relations of the United States, Transmitted to Congress, With the Annual Message of the President, December 1, 1873*, Document 240, history.state.gov.
76. "L'Emigrazione in America," *La Provincia di Pisa*, February 23, 1873, www.internetculturale.it.
77. "Emigrati Italiani," *L'Emancipazione*, January 25, 1873, www.internetculturale.it.
78. *Newcastle Daily Chronicle*, April 16, 1872, British Newspaper Archive, www.britishnewspaperarchive.co.uk.
79. "Neapolitan Emigration and Its Causes," *Leeds Mercury*, November 16, 1872, *British Newspaper Archive*, www.britishnewspaperarchive.co.uk.
80. "Shameful Frauds Upon Italian Emigrants," *Fifeshire Journal*, December 5, 1872, *British Newspaper Archive*, www.britishnewspaperarchive.co.uk.

81. "Parliament—The Italian Minister at Washington," *Scotsman*, February 12, 1873, British Newspaper Archive, www.britishnewspaperarchive.co.uk.

82. "Remarkable Swindle; The Bogus."

83. "Broadway Infested with Italian Beggars," *New York World*, December 18, 1872, www.genealogybank.com.

84. "Emigranti," *L'Emancipazione*, February 17, 1872, www.internetculturale.it.

85. "L'Emigrazione in America."

86. "The Slaves of the Harp," *New York Sun*, September 14, 1872, chroniclingamerica.loc.gov.

87. "White Slave Trade," *New York Tribune*, December 17, 1872, chroniclingamerica.loc.gov.

88. "Italian Cheap Labor: Change in the Methods of the Padrones," *Boston Sunday Herald*, April 7, 1889, 21, www.genealogybank.com.

89. "Landing of Foreign Convicts."

90. "The Defrauded Italians," *New York Sun*, December 18, 1872, chroniclingamerica.loc.gov.

91. "Italians."

92. The figure noted in *Statistica della emigrazione italiana all'estero* is 7,322.

93. U.S. Bureau of the Census, "Migration," 57.

94. Italia: Direzione generale della statistica, *Statistica della emigrazione italiana all'estero* (Rome: Tipografia Bodoniana, 1882), xix, books.google.com.

95. Ibid., xxii–xxxi.

96. *Gazzetta della Provincia di Molise*, August 1; *La Nuova Basilicata*, August 10; *Il Circondario di Barletta*, November 18.

97. "Landing of Foreign Convicts."

98. "Industrie, Arti, e Commercio," *La Nuova Basilicata*, October 26, 1872, www.internetculturale.it.

99. "Giorno per Giorno," *Fanfulla*, May 11, 1872, digitale.bnc.roma.sbn.it.

100. "Discussione del bilancio definitivo pel 1872 del ministero dell'interno," *Rendiconti del Parlamento italiano, Sessione del 1871–1872, Discussioni della Camera dei deputati*, Vol. II (Rome: per gli eredi Botta, 1872), 2,189, books.google.com.

101. Ibid., 2,193.

102. "Emigrazione," *Il Circondario di Barletta*, June 23, 1872, www.internetculturale.it.

103. "Varietà; Emigrazione Italiana," *Il Circondario di Barletta*, June 1, 1871, www.internetculturale.it.

104. "Cronaca Politica," *Fanfulla*, September 12, 1872, digitale.bnc.roma.sbn.it.

105. "Cose di Napoli," *Fanfulla*, July 15, 1872, digitale.bnc.roma.sbn.it.

106. "Nostra Corrispondenza," *L'Emancipazione*, November 9, 1872, www. internetculturale.it.

107. "Emigrazione," *L'Italia Centrale*, April 22, 1873, digilib.netribe.it.

108. "Cronaca Politica," *Fanfulla*, March 12, 1874, digitale.bnc.roma.sbn.it.

109. Ibid.

110. Susan Berglund, "Italian Immigration in Venezuela: A Story Still Untold," in Lydio F. Tomasi, Piero Gastaldo and Thomas Row, *The Columbus People: Perspective in Italian Immigration to the Americas and Australia* (New York: Center for Migration Studies, 1994), 176, books.google.com.

111. "Emigrazione pel Venezuela," *Il Circondario di Barletta*, September 13, 1874, www.internetculturale.it.

112. Ibid.

113. "Cronaca Locale," *Gazzetta della Provincia di Molise*, March 6, 1875, www.internetculturale.it.

114. "Cronaca," *Il Circondario di Barletta*, September 12, 1875, www. internetculturale.it.

115. "Atti Officiali," *Gazzetta della Provincia di Molise*, January 16, 1875, www. internetculturale.it.

116. "Lo Statuto Albertino," *Camera dei Deputati, Parlamento Italiano*, storia. camera.it.

117. The January 3, 1873 *New York Herald* contains statements from some of the *Erin*'s passengers. The article appears in Appendix II.

118. "Italians; More of the Emigration Machinery."

119. See Appendix VIII for details of the study.

120. This illegitimate outfit used the name of the bona fide Pacific Steam Navigation Company of London.

121. "La società di patronato per gli emigranti," *L'Italia Centrale*, April 4, 1876, digilib.netribe.it.

122. Ibid.

123. "The Italian Immigrants," *New York Commercial Advertiser*, December 16, 1872, www.genealogybank.com.

124. "Winter's Carnival," *New York Herald*, December 28, 1872, chroniclingamerica.loc.gov.

125. "Winter Beauties," *New York Herald*, December 29, 1872, chroniclingamerica.loc.gov.

126. "Another Snow-Storm," *New York World*, January 24, 1873, www. genealogybank.com.

127. *New York Sun*, January 28, 1873, chroniclingamerica.loc.gov.

128. "The Weather and the Streets," *New York Evening Post*, February 5, 1873, www.genealogybank.com.

129. "Italian Immigrants," *Harper's Weekly; A Journal of Civilization*, February 1, 1873 (New York: Harper & Brothers, 1873), 98, babel.hathitrust.org.

130. "Burlington and Vicinity," *Burlington Free Press*, December 20, 1872, www.genealogybank.com.

131. "Defrauded Italians."

132. "The Right to Work," *New York Evening Post*, April 10, 1873, www.genealogybank.com.

133. "Immigration," *Richmond Whig*, December 3, 1872, www.genealogybank.com.

134. "An Importation of Brigands," *Charlotte Democrat*, December 24, 1872, www.genealogybank.com.

135. "Defrauded Italians."

136. "Laborers for the Tunnel," *Richmond Daily Dispatch*, December 24, 1872, chroniclingamerica.loc.gov.

137. "Letter from Richmond," *Baltimore Sun*, January 4, 1873, www.genealogybank.com.

138. "Immigration and the Labor Problem," *Staunton Spectator*, January 14, 1873, www.genealogybank.com.

139. "Local Brevities," *Alexandria Gazette*, January 15, 1873, chroniclingamerica.loc.gov.

140. "Italians in Virginia," *Alexandria Gazette*, May 21, 1874, chroniclingamerica.loc.gov.

141. "Will They Strike? The Trades Unions in Motion Once More," *New York Herald*, March 27, 1873, chroniclingamerica.loc.gov.

142. "Another Great Strike Impending," *New York Herald*, March 11, 1873, chroniclingamerica.loc.gov.

143. "The Great Strike," *New York Herald*, June 8, 1872, chroniclingamerica.loc.gov.

144. "Labor Versus Capital; The Impending Strike of the Working Man," *New York Sunday Mercury*, March 23, 1873, www.genealogybank.com.

145. "Is This All Gas?" *New York Herald*, April 9, 1873, chroniclingamerica.loc.gov.

146. "The Moral of the Gas Strike," *New York Herald*, April 8, 1873, chroniclingamerica.loc.gov.

147. "The Gas Famine Ended," *New York Herald*, April 12, 1873, chroniclingamerica.loc.gov.

148. "Labor Movement," *Chicago Daily Tribune*, July 18, 1873, chroniclingamerica.loc.gov.

149. Ibid.

150. Ibid.

151. "Modocery! Murder and Arson at Church Hill," *Mahoning Vindicator*, August 1, 1873, news.google.com.

152. "The Miners' Conspiracy Trial," *New York Herald*, October 4, 1875, www.genealogybank.com.

153. *Labor Tribune*, quoted in "The Italian Miners," *Indianapolis Sentinel*, October 1, 1874, www.genealogybank.com.

154. Robert C. Milici, "The Coalprod Database: Historical Production Data for the Major Coal-Producing Regions of the Conterminous United States," pubs.usgs.gov.

155. Charlotte Erickson, *American Industry and the European Immigrant: 1860–1885* (New York: Russell & Russell, 1967), 84.

156. "Few Miners Are Americans," *New York Sun*, January 24, 1892, chroniclingamerica.loc.gov.

157. "Telegraphic-American Matters," *Daily Phoenix*, August 29, 1873, www.genealogybank.com.

158. "The Proposed Terminus," *Frank Leslie's Illustrated Newspaper*, November 15, 1873, 161–62, www.accessible-archives.com.

159. In December 1871, Grandi and two other investors joined Antonio Meucci to form the *Telettrofono Company*. Meucci received a patent for his "sound telegraph," a device capable of transmitting sound through an electrical wire. Unfortunately, the patent expired in 1874. In 1876, Alexander Graham Bell patented his invention, the telephone.

160. "The Italian Slave Children," *New York Herald*, January 15, 1874, chroniclingamerica.loc.gov.

161. "Co-operative Brooms," *New York Herald*, March 9, 1874, www.genealogybank.com.

162. "The Associated Laborers," *New York Commercial Advertiser*, March 12, 1874, www.genealogybank.com.

163. "A Plea for the Italian Laborers," *New York Tribune*, June 24, 1874, chroniclingamerica.loc.gov.

164. "Italian Workmen," *New York Evening Post*, July 22, 1874, www.genealogybank.com.

165. Ibid.

166. "New York," Memphis *Public Ledger*, June 24, 1874, chroniclingamerica.loc.gov.

167. "Plea for the Italian Laborers."

168. Of the nearly 3,000 swindled Italians, 200 left in 1873 for mines in Coalburg and Church Hill, Ohio. Some of the 231 hired in 1872 for Richmond's Church Hill tunnel returned to New York.

169. "Co-operative Italian Laborers," *Cleveland Leader*, July 3, 1874, www.genealogybank.com.

170. Herbert G. Gutman, "The Buena Vista Affair, 1874–1875," *Pennsylvania Magazine of History and Biography* 88, no. 3 (July 1964): 255–56, journals.psu.edu.

171. "The Miners' Strike," *New York Herald*, September 26, 1874, chroniclingamerica.loc.gov.

172. "The Miners' Version," *Washington* (PA) *Review and Examiner*, October 7, 1874, www.genealogybank.com.

173. *Cincinnati Daily Gazette*, September 30, 1874, www.genealogybank.com.

174. "The Youghiogheny Murder," *Pittsburgh Gazette,* December 1, 1874, news.google.com.

175. For her bravery, King Victor Emmanuel II awarded Annie the *medaglia al valor civile*, medal of civil valor, "as an award for courageous and philanthropic actions."

176. "General News Summary," *Harrisburg Daily Patriot*, December 17, 1875, www.genealogybank.com.

177. "The Colored Miners," *Wheeling Register*, May 12, 1882, chroniclingamerica.loc.gov.

178. "The Italian Must Go," *Boston Daily Advertiser*, April 10, 1882, www.genealogybank.com.

Chapter 3

179. Giovanni Florenzano, *Della emigrazione italiana in America comparata alle altre emigrazioni europee* (Naples: Tipi di F. Giannini, 1874), 169, books.google.com.

180. "L'Emigrazione," *Il Commercio Savonese*, February 18, 1873, bibliotecadigitale.regione.liguria.it.

181. "L'Emigrazione in America."

182. "L'Emigrazione," *Il Secolo*, January 27, 1873, fsu.digital.flvc.org.

183. "Landing of Foreign Convicts," 50.

184. "Italy, Emigration to America," *Boston Pilot*, December 20, 1873, newspapers.bc.edu.

185. "Emigrazione," *La Libertá*, May 12, 1877, www.internetculturale.it.

186. "L'Emigrazione Italiana," *L'Italia Centrale*, November 22, 1877, digilib. netribe.it.

187. *Atti del parlamento italiano, camera dei deputati, XIII Legislatura, Sessione del 1876–1877, Discussioni, Vol. V, Dal 22 novembre 1877 al 23 gennaio 1878* (Roma: per gli Eredi Botta, 1878), 5,036, storia.camera.it.

188. *Atti parlamentari della camera senatori, Discussioni, Legislatura XII, Sessione 1874-1875, Vol. II,* (Roma: Cotta E. Comp, 1875), 1,132, books.google.com.

189. Nicotera, a member of the leftist party, freely admitted the failure of his antecedents, Lanza and Cantelli, both members of the political right.

190. Excerpts of these proposals can be found in Appendix X.

191. Italia: Direzione generale della statistica, *Statistica della emigrazione italiana all'estero* (Rome: Tipografia Bodoniana, 1882), 42, books.google.com.

192. Ibid., 44.

193. "White Slaves in Gotham: the Italian Padroni and Their Victims," *Harrisburg State Journal*, August 30, 1884, www.genealogybank.com.

194. "Signor Baccari's Italians," *New York Tribune*, June 4, 1882, chroniclingamerica.loc.gov.

195. Ibid.

196. Ibid.

197. "Attacking a Nefarious System," *New York Tribune*, December 17, 1884, chroniclingamerica.loc.gov.

198. "Italians as Railway-Builders. Scenes on the West Shore Road," *Frank Leslie's Illustrated Newspaper*, October 14, 1882, www.accessible-archives. com.

199. Ibid.

200. "Rise of Industrial America, 1876–1900," Library of Congress, www. loc.gov.

201. "Italian Slavery; How the Immigrants Are Brought Over Under Long Contracts with Bosses," *Wheeling Register*, September 11, 1883, chroniclingamerica.loc.gov.

202. "Miscellaneous," *New York Tribune*, April 1, 1897, chroniclingamerica. loc.gov.

203. "Importation of Contract Laborers, Etc.," *Testimony Taken by the Select Committee of the House of Representatives to Inquire into the Alleged Violation of the Laws Prohibiting the Importation of Contract Laborers, Paupers, Convicts, and Other Classes* (Washington, D.C.: Government Printing Office, 1888), 33–35, babel.hathitrust.org.

204. Excerpts from some of these interviews appear in Appendix III.

205. Appendix IV contains excerpts from the reports of Powderly and Schulteis.

206. "Immigration Investigation," *Report of the Select Committee on Immigration and Naturalization* (Washington, D.C.: Government Printing Office, 1891), 507, babel.hathitrust.org.

207. Ibid., 360.

208. Ibid.

209. Ibid.

210. "Cheap Labor," *Youngstown Vindicator*, March 1, 1902, news.google.com.

211. "Labor and Wages," *Engineering and Mining Journal* 38 (October 4, 1884): 233, babel.hathitrust.org.

212. Florenzano, *Della emigrazione italiana in America*, 155.

213. "Comprachicos. The Traffic in Italian Children in Europe and America," *New York Herald*, August 25, 1873, chroniclingamerica.loc.gov.

214. "Give the Honors to the Right Man," *New York Sun*, March 26, 1875, chroniclingamerica.loc.gov.

215. *La Crónica*, April 7, 1875, chroniclingamerica.loc.gov.

216. "He Was with Custer," *New North-west*, October 29, 1886, chroniclingamerica.loc.gov.

Epilogue

217. U.S. Bureau of the Census, "Migration," 57.

218. Mark I. Choate, *Emigrant Nation: The Making of Italy Abroad* (Cambridge, MA: Harvard University Press, 2008), 1, books.google.com.

219. "Miscellaneous Notes," *Austin Weekly Statesman*, September 4, 1884, chroniclingamerica.loc.gov.

Appendix III

220. "Importation of Contract Laborers," 114–38.

Appendix IV

221. "Letter from the Secretary of the Treasury," *Letter from the Secretary of the Treasury, Transmitting a Report of the Commissioners of Immigration Upon the*

Causes Which Incite Immigration to the United States, Vol. 1 (Washington, D.C.: Government Printing Office, 1892), 11, babel.hathitrust.org.

222. "Report of Commissioner Joseph Powderly," *Letter from the Secretary of the Treasury, Transmitting a Report of the Commissioners of Immigration Upon the Causes Which Incite Immigration to the United States*, Vol. 1 (Washington, D.C.: Government Printing Office, 1892), 246–57, babel.hathitrust.org.

223. "Report of Commissioner H.J. Schulteis," *Letter from the Secretary of the Treasury, Transmitting a Report of the Commissioners of Immigration Upon the Causes Which Incite Immigration to the United States*, Vol. 1 (Washington, D.C.: Government Printing Office, 1892), 263–300, babel.hathitrust.org.

Appendix V

224. "Remarkable Swindle."

Appendix VI

225. "Landing of Foreign Convicts," 49.

Appendix IX

226. "New York Passenger Lists, 1820–1891," Family Search, www.familysearch.org.

Appendix X

227. *Atti del parlamento italiano, camera dei deputati, II della XIII Legislatura, Sessione del 1878, Discussioni, Vol. II, Dal 13 maggio 1878 al 17 giugno 1878 inclusivo* (Roma: per gli Eredi Botta, 1878), 1,506–8, storia.camera.it.

INDEX

ABOUT THE AUTHORS

Joe Tucciarone was born in Youngstown, Ohio. He earned a bachelor of science degree from Youngstown State University and a master's degree from the University of Toledo. In 2000, he was awarded an honorary doctorate of science from Youngstown State University. His astronomical animations have appeared in dozens of Discovery and National Geographic Channel documentaries, and he has illustrated the covers of several books, including *When the Sun Dies* and *Night Comes to the Cretaceous*. Joe's article "The First Italians in Trumbull County, Ohio," was published in *La Gazzetta Italiana Newspaper*.

Ben Lariccia, a native of Youngstown, writes on Italian American history. He has a bachelor's degree from the University of Dayton and a master's degree in bilingual/bicultural education from La Salle University. For thirty years, he taught in the School District of Philadelphia. Ben is a contributing writer at *La Gazzetta Italiana Newspaper*. His work is also published in print and online by the Italian group Amici di Capracotta. He is a member of the America-Italy Society of Philadelphia and the Italian American Studies Association. In 2019, The History Press released Joe and Ben's *Coal War in the Mahoning Valley: The Origin of Greater Youngstown's Italians*.